The Rise and Fall
of Communism

#5763

Robert Charles.
April 1993
Goshen. IN.

The Rise and Fall of Communism

Richard H. Hudelson
The University of Minnesota, Duluth

Westview Press
BOULDER • SAN FRANCISCO • OXFORD

Copyright © 1993 by Westview Press, Inc.

Published in 1993 in the United States of America by Westview Press, Inc., 5500 Central Avenue, Boulder, Colorado 80301-2877, and in the United Kingdom by Westview Press, 36 Lonsdale Road, Summertown, Oxford OX2 7EW

Library of Congress Cataloging-in-Publication Data
Hudelson, Richard.
    The rise and fall of communism / Richard H. Hudelson.
        p. cm.
    Includes bibliographical references and index.
    ISBN 0-8133-1559-X. --ISBN 0-8133-1560-3 (pbk.)
        1. Communism--History--20th century. 2. Socialism--History--
20th century. I. Title.
HX40.H738   1993
335.43'09'04--dc20   92 - 35855
                                                                                    CIP

Printed and bound in the United States of America

The paper used in this publication meets the requirements
of the American National Standard for Permanence of Paper
for Printed Library Materials Z39.48-1984.

10   9   8   7   6   5   4   3   2   1

To Eileen

Contents

Acknowledgments

Writing this book has been a rewarding but challenging experience. Along the way I have had the helpful comments and criticisms of a number of friends and colleagues. Pat Maus, Susanna Frenkel, Kit Christensen, and Carl Ross read the entire manuscript. Steve Chilton, Milan Kovacovic, and Marina Rumyantseva read parts of it. They and the reviewers for Westview Press have weeded out many errors and forced me to think through a number of difficult points. The errors and confusions that remain do so in spite of their best efforts. I thank them all. I would also like to thank Spencer Carr of Westview Press for his support of this project and for his editorial suggestions, which resulted in major improvements. Finally, thanks to Jean Vileta for her editorial assistance in preparing the manuscript for publication.

This book deals with highly controversial material. The views expressed are my own. They rest on my thought and experience. The differing opinions of those whom I know to be honest and thoughtful readers have driven home to me the largeness of the issues and the limits of our thought.

Richard H. Hudelson

Introduction

In this twentieth century we human beings have achieved both great and terrible things. Our technology dwarfs the achievements of the past. But our depravity, too, stands magnified by the increased powers at our disposal. Ours is the century of spaceflight and the century of the holocaust. Perhaps neither better nor worse than the human beings who have preceded us, nonetheless we cut a wider path.

Communism, the grand experiment that spans the century from near beginning to end, exhibits this same mixture of greatness and depravity. Rooted in a nineteenth-century dream of universal human emancipation, the communist cause called forth heroism and saintliness but also cruelty and servility. A history of communism would tell us much about the century we occupy and about ourselves as well.

For over a century, dreams of a better world inspired tens of thousands of human beings from around the globe to dedicate their lives to the cause of socialism. The experiment in communism, which began in Russia with the Bolshevik revolution in 1917, grew out of this broader international socialist movement. The dramatic collapse of communism in Eastern Europe and the former Soviet Union heralds the failure of this great experiment. But what does this failure mean? Does it prove that socialism cannot work? Does it show that the vision of universal human emancipation is a phantasm that we must now abandon? What are we to make of the rise and of the fall of communism?

These are the questions that lie behind this work. They are philosophical questions, but they are philosophical questions that cannot be addressed in the absence of some understanding of the historical process that gave rise to them. According to one popular conception, a philosophical wall separates the vision of communism from the vision of socialism. In fact, throughout the nineteenth century "communism" and "socialism" were pretty much synonymous terms. It was not until the split in the international socialist movement, following the Bolshevik revolution of 1917, that "communism" and "socialism" took on distinct meanings. From this point on "communists" were socialists who followed the ideas of the Bolshevik leader V. I. Lenin, and "socialists" were socialists who did not. At bottom, what separated communists and socialists was not so much distinct philosophical conceptions of the future society they aimed to create as differences about the steps necessary to reach this future society. To be sure, communist convictions about the steps necessary for constructing socialism significantly affected the version of socialism built in the Soviet Union and elsewhere, but for socialists and communists alike the ultimate goal was a society in which rational cooperation replaced marketplace competition as the governing principle of social life.

There are many who do see in the fall of communism in Eastern Europe and the Soviet Union definite proof of the inevitable failure of all forms of socialism. But there are others who do not draw this conclusion. They argue that Soviet communism, which was widely copied in Eastern Europe, was a fundamentally flawed version of socialism. For them, the failure of Soviet communism does not prove the failure of all possible forms of socialism.

In order to think through this controversy, it is necessary to have some understanding of the particular version of socialism that was developed in the Soviet Union and Eastern Europe and of its relationship to the socialist tradition from which it grew. And to achieve this understanding, it is necessary to have some understanding of the historical choices that were made. Is the failure of the Soviet experiment due to perversions of Soviet socialism introduced by Joseph Stalin? Was the 1917 Bolshevik revolution, under the leadership of Lenin, from the beginning a betrayal of socialism, as many prominent socialists argued at the time? Or do the seeds of the failure of Soviet communism lie deeper, in the ideas of Karl Marx and Frederick Engels that came to dominate the socialist movement in the late nineteenth century? Can we find among pre-Marxist visions of socialism the model for a viable socialist future? None of these is simply a historical question, but none of them can be answered without a sense of the history from which it is drawn.

This work aims at providing an introductory history of the socialist movement. Although it was written with an eye to questions about the philosophical significance of the rise and fall of communism, it offers a straightforward historical account that should be of value to all who are not specialists in the field. Its subject matter is the course of the international socialist movement from its origins in the early nineteenth century to the present.

This said, several qualifications are in order. First, the reader will discover that American communism has received attention out of proportion to its significance in the worldwide communist movement. The only reason for this emphasis is that I am an American writing for an American audience.

Second, the reader should be clear that this work is not intended as a history of the Soviet Union. The Soviet Union is a product of diverse historical forces of which the socialist movement is only one. There are even some historians who think that the socialist movement is largely irrelevant to understanding the history of the Soviet Union. Although I would not go so far as this, I would agree that other factors may have been more important than the socialist movement in shaping the Soviet experience. But it is only as an experiment in communism, a particular version of socialism, that the Soviet Union interests me here. In this work the central question is what the fall of Soviet communism means for the cause of socialism.

Third, it should be kept in mind that this work is intended only as an introductory history of the socialist movement. There is some truth in the historian's claim that "God lives in the details." If God is truth, then truth, the full truth, demands our respect for the details of the narrative. But it is also true that our mortal minds cannot comprehend all the details. We require some schema in order to have any understanding at all of the world around us. It is only in light of such a schema that we can begin to approach the details, questioning them for their true significance and altering our schema in light of them. This work aims at providing an introductory overview that can make possible a fruitful examination of the details.

Finally, it will become apparent to the reader that, although sometimes deeply critical, I sympathize with what socialists and communists have tried to do. Other fair-minded people may see things quite differently. Given the aim of the work, its brevity, and the controversial nature of the subject matter, it is almost inevitable that specialists in the various fields upon which this work touches will find serious omissions or distortions in the material at hand. Recognizing that this is so, nonetheless I would like to make clear that throughout this work I have aimed at the truth. I do not subscribe to the currently fashionable view that objective truth is an illusion. Here I shall not attempt to defend my belief in the possibility of such a truth.[1] I shall record only that it has been my aim.

---

1. In *Marxism and Philosophy in the Twentieth Century* (New York: Praeger, 1990), I do address such issues.

1

Origins of the
Working-class Movement

Capitalism is a way of life. It is a way of life that we in the United States take for granted. In a capitalist system, private entrepreneurs advance a certain amount of capital. With this capital they build, buy, or rent production facilities, purchase raw materials, and hire laborers to work for them. The finished product is sold on the open market, and the income from the sale of the product returns to the entrepreneur who started it all. The entrepreneur consumes a part of this income and the rest is used to repeat the productive process anew, to expand the process of production, or to begin a new productive venture.

This way of life presupposes a number of institutions. It presupposes the existence of entrepreneurs in possession of sufficient capital to begin the production process. It presupposes the availability of production facilities and raw materials that can be purchased or rented. It presupposes the availability of workers willing to sell their labor power for a fixed duration of time. It presupposes the existence of markets in which the means of production, labor time, and finished products can be purchased or sold. And it presupposes a stable political structure strong enough to protect and maintain the property rights of buyers and sellers in these markets.

In a capitalist system individuals depend on other people to produce the goods and services each needs to survive. Survival depends on the ability of these individuals to exchange the goods each has to sell for the goods each needs to survive. Production is production for sale. Each producer specializes in some particular product: food, blankets, shoes, or bicycles, for example. And within the production process itself, each worker specializes in some particular task: tanning the leather, cutting the leather, sewing the seams, or attaching the soles or heels of shoes, for example. Adam Smith, the great champion of capitalism as a way of life, saw in this division of labor the potential for an enormous increase in human wealth. He wrote, "The greatest improvement in the productive powers of labour, and the greater part of the skill, dexterity, and judgment with which it is any where directed, or applied, seem to have been the effects of the division of labour."[1] This division of labor is impossible without the existence of some system for exchanging products. Within a capitalist system of production, competitive markets provide the institutional structure that makes such exchange possible. Within such markets the exchange ratios between various products, their relative prices, are regulated by the forces of demand and supply. Neither individual buyers nor individual sellers can set the prices for commodities bought or sold. Each must accept the market price. "The market price of every particular commodity is regulated by the proportion between the quantity which is actually brought to market, and the demand of those who are willing to pay."[2]

Adam Smith thought that production for sale within such competitive markets worked to reduce the price of every commodity to the lowest possible level. He contrasted the price of a commodity monopolized by one seller with the prices of commodities sold under conditions of competition between sellers:

> The price of monopoly is upon every occasion the highest which can be got. The natural price, or the price of free competition, on the contrary, is the lowest which can be taken, not upon every occasion indeed, but for any considerable time together. The one is upon every occasion the highest which can be squeezed out of the buyers, or which, it is supposed, they will consent to give: The other is the lowest which the sellers can commonly afford to take, and at the same time continue their business.[3]

A seller may upon some occasion secure a price higher than that necessary to sustain his or her business. If, for example, an entrepreneur discovers a more efficient way to produce shoes, then that entrepreneur's unit costs of production will be lower than average, and hence the entrepreneur could afford to sell beneath the market price. This lower unit cost gives the entrepreneur leeway as to how to price the product. Either the price can be set at the market price, in which case the entrepreneur secures greater-than-average profits, or the price can be set

---

1.   Adam Smith, *An Inquiry into the Nature and Causes of the Wealth of Nations* (New York: Modern Library, 1937), p. 3.

2.   Ibid., p. 56.

3.   Ibid., p. 61.

at below-market prices, in which case competing producers will be forced to lower their prices or face extinction. In either case, competitive pressures will force an adjustment in supply and in the market price of the commodity produced. If the product is sold at below-market prices, producers who cannot meet the competition of lower prices will drop out of the industry, and the market price will fall to a level that is the lowest that sellers can commonly afford to take. If the product is sold at the market price with resulting higher-than-average profits, entrepreneurs will be attracted into the industry, the supply of the commodity will increase, and consequently, the price will fall to the lowest level sellers can afford. It is in this sense then that prices in competitive markets are, as Smith says, "for any considerable time together," the lowest possible prices for the commodities produced.

This example of the effects of the discovery of a more efficient technique of production illustrates three interesting features of competitive markets. The first feature is the tendency of prices in such markets to gravitate toward the lowest possible price sellers can afford. A second feature is the self-regulative capacity of such competitive markets. Changes in production techniques, in the supply of raw materials, or in the demand for consumer goods automatically induce corrections in the quantities of particular commodities produced, and in the prices of these commodities, thus achieving a new equilibrium around the lowest price sellers can afford. Third, the example illustrates an incentive to innovation inherent in the pressures of competitive markets. Each producer has an incentive to come up with more efficient techniques of production--for the discovery of such techniques lowers the unit costs of production for that producer and makes possible a higher-than-average rate of profit for that producer. To be sure, this advantage is temporary. Eventually competitors will adopt the new and more efficient techniques, and the price of the commodity will fall. But even temporary advantages result in a greater accumulation of wealth, and incentives remain to seek out other production efficiencies as well. Since these incentives work on every producer, the result is a systematic tendency of competitive markets to encourage innovation and greater efficiency in the process of production.

Capitalism is a way of life that has not always been with us. It has a relatively late appearance in the history of humankind. Before capitalism, for a period of roughly one thousand years between the fall of the Roman Empire and the emergence of capitalism, life in Europe was organized according to the system of feudalism. Under feudalism, the land was divided into large estates, which belonged to the church, the crown, or members of the feudal aristocracy. These estates were, for the most part, preserved and passed intact with the death of one feudal lord to an eldest son or nearest male relative. The ruling lord was surrounded by a system of subordinate nobles, some of whom were granted control over parts of the higher lord's estate or held control over smaller estates of their own. The feudal aristocracy was organized into a pyramidal structure of relations of service and subordination. At the bottom of the feudal class structure, beneath the aristocracy, was the peasantry, a class that included the vast majority of the people of feudal Europe. The peasants lived in villages on the feudal estates. They farmed the land, both in plots allotted to their own use and in the fields of the feudal lord. From time to time they were also called upon to help in the building of roads and fortifications and in the performance of whatever other work might be required to maintain the estate.

Life in feudalism differed in many ways from life in capitalism. In the feudal system almost all production was done for local consumption. Trade, exchange, and markets were not central to the provision of the bulk of the goods necessary for consumption and renewed production. As late as the early part of the twentieth century, remnants of the feudal nobility in Russia continued to pride themselves on the self-sufficiency of their estates. Unlike the wage laborers of capitalism who sell their labor power on the open market and are free to travel wherever they like in search of better pay or a better job, feudal peasants were legally bound to the estate of their birth. They performed work for the feudal lord, not in exchange for wage payment, but in response to the direct coercive threat of the ruling aristocracy. For the most part, peasants lived and died on the estates of their birth. The tasks they performed were predominantly agricultural or directly related to the requirements of agriculture. Production and the way of life organized around the tasks of production remained largely the same for generation after generation. In contrast to the dynamic, innovative character of capitalism, feudalism was characterized by a repetitive and static way of life.

There was no single cause responsible for the transformation from feudalism to capitalism in Western Europe. No attempt will be made here to explain that transformation.[4] But whatever the ultimate causes,

---

4. For attempts to understand this change, see Karl Marx, *Capital*, vol. 1, part 8, "The So Called Primitive Accumulation" (1867) (New York: International, 1973), pp. 713-760; Karl Polanyi, *The Great Transformation* (Boston: Beacon Press, 1957); Maurice Dobb, *Studies in the Development of Capitalism* (New York: International, 1947); and Fernand Braudel, *Capitalism and Material Life, 1400-1800* (New York: Harper and Row, 1973). The recent work of Robert Brenner has provoked a stimulating debate. On this see T. H. Aston and C.H.E.

the transformation involved at least the following factors. First, there appeared a class of what might be called protocapitalists. For the most part, these protocapitalists did not come from the landed nobility. Instead, they emerged from the ranks of medieval merchants and artisans who had established themselves in various European cities where they had some independence from the domination of the landed aristocracy. Second, there appeared also a class of wage laborers available to be employed by the protocapitalists. These wage laborers came from two distinct groups. Some were artisans and apprentices who, because of the breakdown of the feudal guilds, were in need of gainful employment. Others were peasants forced off the estates of the landed nobility.

Capitalism began with the development of a system of manufacturing in which protocapitalists paid wages in exchange for the use of the labor power of these dispossessed peasants and artisans and then sold the commodities produced in open markets that had developed in the cities as a result of increasing trade. In its earliest forms this system of manufacturing involved simply this change in the organization of production. The technology employed remained the same as the technology employed in earlier times. In many cases workers were not even united under one roof. The key change turned on the introduction of wage labor as the relation of production connecting workers and capitalists. Subsequent to the introduction of this system of manufactures, several factors--increasing division of labor, technological innovation, and the bringing together of workers into large and interconnected facilities for production--vastly increased the productive powers of labor and started the capitalist system on the road to a revolutionary transformation of life in Western Europe.

With its inherently dynamic character and productive efficiency, capitalism pushed aside the old feudal ways of life. With the spread of capitalism went the growth of the distinctive social classes of capitalism: the owners of capital (the bourgeoisie) and the free sellers of labor power (the proletariat). The bourgeoisie, this growing class of wealthy and enterprising men, included many individuals who were not of the hereditary nobility. They were excluded from positions of political power reserved for members of the nobility. In addition, numerous restrictions imposed by and in the interests of the nobility hampered their business ventures, whereas a patchwork of special privileges and

Philpin, eds., *The Brenner Debate: Agrarian Class Structure and Economic Development in Pre-Industrial Europe* (Cambridge: Cambridge University Press, 1985).

benefits, paid for by taxes imposed on the rising bourgeoisie, showered down on the ruling aristocracy. In a relatively short period of time the rising bourgeoisie demanded an elimination of the privileged status of the nobility and an equal share in political power. The result was a contest for political power between the feudal aristocracy and the newly created bourgeoisie. In England this contest, complicated by a clash between conflicting religious sects, led through civil war and dictatorship to the "glorious revolution" of 1688 in which the ascendancy of the bourgeoisie was established. One hundred years later this same conflict led to the great French Revolution, to civil war, and to revolutionary war throughout much of Western Europe.

The revolutionary bourgeoisie proclaimed the natural equality of all men and the consequent equality of rights belonging to all men by nature. It demanded that careers be open to talent rather than reserved for the nobility. And it demanded the subordination of kings and the hereditary nobility to parliaments elected by the people. Capitalism, in which each individual is free to trade as he sees fit and in which the will of political superiors is replaced by the market forces of supply and demand, seemed well suited to the needs of free and equal men. And in lowering prices and increasing output capitalism held the potential for making men rich as well as free. Adam Smith had argued that the framework of capitalism served as an "invisible hand" by which the effort of each to secure his own happiness was turned to the benefit of society as a whole.[5] Smith's argument came after capitalism had firmly taken root and after the political struggle for power in England. But in showing how capitalism contained within it the prospect of increasing wealth for all, Smith linked utilitarian considerations for the happiness of all with the revolutionary appeal to natural equality and natural rights that had accompanied the rise of capitalism. The result was the powerful ideology of classical liberalism that saw in capitalism both the realization of human freedom and the prospect of human happiness.

In his tempered and rational optimism Adam Smith personified the spirit of the Enlightenment, which proclaimed both the emancipation of humankind from its past and the bright prospects of its future. But if Adam Smith saw in capitalism the vision of a better world, others found in it a nightmarish degradation of human life. As we have seen, capitalism required the existence of a class of free laborers who offered their labor power for sale. These wage laborers, the proletariat, did not appear out of nowhere. The great bulk of them were farmers who had

---

5.   Smith, *Inquiry*, p. 423.

been forced off the land. In England, which became the leading center of the development of capitalism, most of the population in the late fourteenth and early fifteenth centuries lived as small farmers on land to which they had some right of use deriving from the traditions of feudal law. From the fifteenth to the seventeenth centuries many of these people were driven off their land. The feudal lords, hard pressed for cash, began to convert the land from the production of grain for human consumption to game preserves and sheep farms that produced wool for sale. This enclosure movement, which involved fencing off the land for sheep, brought also the conversion of farmed land into pastures and the destruction of peasant homes, villages, and churches. Repeated attempts were made to stem the tide of enclosures by royal decree.[6] But the nobility's need for cash prevailed, and by 1750 the small farmer had largely disappeared from the English countryside.

However curtailed his rights may have been in feudal times, the common peasant at least had access to the land he needed to grow his food and to a house to shelter his family. With the enclosure movement the peasant farmer was deprived of his house and cut off from the land that had heretofore provided his means of survival. Thus liberated from feudal ways, large numbers of these dispossessed rural folk roamed the English countryside, some begging, some in search of work, and some as bandits. Beginning with the reign of Henry VII (1485-1509), laws were passed designed to curtail this vagabondage. According to an act of Henry VIII (passed in 1530), beggars old and unable to work were to be granted licenses to beg. Those able to work were to be "tied to the cart-tail and whipped until the blood streams from their bodies, then to swear an oath to go back to their birthplace or to where they have lived the last three years and to put themselves to labor."[7] Later, the act was strengthened to include provisions for second and third arrests for vagabondage. "For the second arrest for vagabondage the whipping is to be repeated and half the ear sliced off; but for the third relapse the offender is to be executed as a hardened criminal and enemy of the common weal."[8] During the reign of Henry VIII, 72,000 of these people were hanged.[9] Subsequent legislation provided for condemning these vagabonds as temporary slaves to anyone willing to feed them and put them to work. Various of these laws provided for branding or executing

---

6. Marx, *Capital*, vol. 1, pp. 719-721.
7. Ibid., p. 734.
8. Ibid., pp. 734-735.
9. Karl Marx, *The German Ideology* (New York: International, 1966), p. 51.

runaways and for putting these "slaves" in irons, chains, or iron rings around the neck, arms, or legs. The laws also provided that the children of vagabonds were to be taken from them and turned over as "apprentices" to those who would put them to work.[10]

In this way, by the combined forces of need and legal terror, the dispossessed rural people were herded into the new manufacturing enterprises that were in growing need of wage laborers. Such a forced transition from an agricultural way of life, governed by the traditions of the village and the rhythms of nature, to life as a wage laborer in a manufacturing enterprise, governed by the disciplined routine imposed by competitive markets, was bound to have a traumatic effect on these people. Their plight was made even worse by the conditions of life they found in these emerging industries.

In the first place, the length of the working day was extended. In agriculture, of course, the length of the working day is variable, depending on the seasons and the tasks at hand. In the new manufacturing enterprises the working day grew to fourteen, sixteen, and even eighteen hours per day. With the development of large manufacturing facilities, thousands of wage laborers crowded into the growing factory towns. There they worked and lived in cramped, dirty, and poorly lighted spaces. Their working places were often badly polluted with dust or noxious fumes. In these places they were forced to work at breakneck speed, standing throughout the long working day surrounded by dangerous machinery. The streets around their homes were unpaved. They flowed with mud and with the sewage of human wastes and the wastes of animals people tried to maintain in these new conditions. They suffered chronic health problems--particularly respiratory problems--and many of them died at an early age from disease or simply from exhaustion caused by poor nutrition and overwork. In the early days of capitalism, the demand for wage laborers exceeded the supply. To prevent competitive pressures from forcing wages up, laws were passed limiting the wages that could be paid. Wage rates were set in such a way that a single paycheck was insufficient to support a family. In order to earn enough for families to survive, it became necessary for women and children to enter the mines and mills alongside the adult men. Children were often beaten for falling asleep, failing to produce according to norms, or for spoiling a piece of work. Under such conditions, family life decayed. Alcoholism and drug use became avenues of escape for men, women, and children. Crime,

---

10. Marx, *Capital*, vol. 1, pp. 735-736.

prostitution, illegitimacy, and child slavery became common. The emerging industrial working class dwelt in a world of slums and factories new to England that was not served by educational, cultural, and religious institutions.

Some sense of what life was like for these people is provided by this statement by Ann Eggley, an eighteen-year-old worker in a coal mine:

I'm sure I don't know how to spell my name. We go at four in the morning, and sometimes at half-past four. We begin to work as soon as we get down. We get out after four, sometimes at five, in the evening. We work the whole time except an hour for dinner, and sometimes we haven't time to eat. I hurry [pull a load of coal from where it was dug to the main shaft where it would be taken to the surface] by myself and have done so for long. I know the corves [basket or box filled with coal] are very heavy, they are the biggest corves anywhere about. The work is far too hard for me; the sweat runs off me all over sometimes. I am very tired at night. Sometimes when we get home at night we have not power to wash us, and then we go to bed. Sometimes we fall asleep in the chair. Father said last night it was both a shame and a disgrace for girls to work as we do, but there is naught else for us to do. I began to hurry when I was seven and I have been hurrying ever since. I have been 11 years in the pits. The girls are always tired. I was poorly twice this winter; it was with the headache. I hurry for Robert Wiggins [the man who dug the coal]; he is not akin to me. . . . We don't always get enough to eat and drink, but we get a good supper. I have known my father go at two in the morning to work . . . and he didn't come out till four. I am quite sure that we work constantly 12 hours except on Saturdays. We wear trousers and our shifts in the pit and great big shoes clinkered and nailed. The girls never work naked to the waist in our pit. The men don't insult us in the pit. The conduct of the girls in the pit is good enough sometimes and sometimes bad enough. I never went to day-school. I went a little to a Sunday-school, but I soon gave it over. I thought it too bad to be confined both Sundays and week-days. I walk about and get the fresh air on Sundays. I have not learnt to read. I don't know my letters. I never learnt naught. I never go to church or chapel; there is no church or chapel at Gawber, there is none nearer than a mile. . . . I have never heard that a good man came into the world who was God's son to save sinners. I never heard of Christ at all. Nobody has ever told me about him, nor have my father and mother ever taught me to pray. I know no prayer: I never pray.[11]

11. Testimony before the Ashley Mines Commission of the British Parliament (1842), in John Bowditch and Clement Ramsland, eds., *Voices of the Industrial Revolution* (Ann Arbor: University of Michigan, 1978), pp. 87-88. Other views of the life of the English

This testimony is not untypical of early English working class experience. No doubt life was hard for these people. But it was even worse for those who could not find a job. By the nineteenth century the growth in demand for wage laborers had slowed relative to the growing supply of people looking for work. Unemployment became a serious problem for large numbers of people. As early as the reign of Elizabeth (1558-1603), taxes had been levied to pay for the upkeep of people unable to work. In 1834 a new poor law was passed that provided for workhouses to which the unemployed poor were to be sent. "Our intention," said one assistant commissioner, "is to make the workhouses as like prisons as possible." Another administrator said, "Our object . . . is to establish therein a discipline so severe and repulsive as to make them a terror to the poor and prevent them from entering."[12] Diet was reduced to a minimum. Personal effects were taken from the inmates. Men and women were separated and same sex members of the same family were separated from one another. A rigid schedule, labor, and total confinement in the workhouse were enforced. By 1843 the population in these workhouses had risen to nearly 200,000. Only desperate people would go to such places. As E. P. Thompson observed, "The most eloquent testimony to the depths of poverty [outside the workhouses] is in the fact that they were tenanted at all."[13]

The spread of slums, beggars, paupers, prostitutes, and criminals did not go entirely unnoticed by the upper and middle classes. Although many blamed the plight of the poor on their own sloth, lust, or base characters, many others spoke out against the new system that had so hideously transformed the English land and the English people. The poets William Blake, William Wordsworth, Samuel Taylor Coleridge, and Percy Bysshe Shelley, lamented the barren values of the times and called for a radical transformation that would fulfill the vision of the biblical prophets and the hopes of the French revolutionaries. The journalist and Chartist, William Cobbett, contrasted the pleasures and

---

working class can be found in *Tess of the d'Urbervilles* by Thomas Hardy and in the novels of Charles Dickens. Flora Tristan, *London Journal* (1840); Frederick Engels, *Condition of the Working Class in England* (1844); and Karl Marx, *Capital* (1867,) vol. 1, chapter 15, "Machinery and Modern Industry" provide first-hand accounts of working-class life in the nineteenth century. E. P. Thompson, *The Making of the English Working Class* (1963), provides a rich historical account of English working-class experience.

12.   Both quotations are from E. P. Thompson, *The Making of the English Working Class* (New York: Vintage, 1966), p. 267.

13.   Ibid., p. 268.

virtues of the vanishing rural England with the misery and moral collapse of the emerging capitalist order. The same themes of loss of traditional Christian virtues and of contemporary moral failure run through essays of John Ruskin and Thomas Carlyle.

Both the romantic poets and the essayists looked on the England of their time with a divided consciousness. On the one hand, they deplored the degeneration of their times and in this sense looked back to an older, more virtuous, and more noble time, when human beings were tied to one another by bonds of duty, community, and friendship and not just by self-interested contracts. On the other hand, they looked forward to a future that would elevate humankind beyond anything ever before seen in history. Neither the poets nor the essayists had any clear blueprint for the society of the future. The poets, at least during the early stages of the French Revolution, adopted a democratic stance that looked to the overthrow of all ruling classes. Later, Carlyle and Ruskin called on the upper classes to reform themselves and provide the moral leadership necessary to restore England to virtue and return happiness to its people. Perhaps the most widely read and most vivid picture of the wretched conditions afflicting the English working class was provided in the novels of Charles Dickens. But whereas Dickens routinely saved his heroes by the device of discovering that they had been born into a more elevated station in life and arranging for them to be restored to it, this solution was not universally available to the working class. Consequently, it is no wonder that members of the working class began to search for ways by which they themselves might struggle against their masters and their conditions of life.

The American and French revolutions profoundly affected the working class movement in England and the rest of Europe. In England an awakening of sorts had already spread throughout parts of the working class in the revivalism of the Methodists and Baptists in the eighteenth century. While the religious revivalists such as Wesley preached subservience to political rulers, they also preached about the need for individual redemption. And in reaching out to the unchurched working class, they affirmed the human worth of every Englishman. The revivalist vision of heaven and hell and the need for rebirth, a radical change in being, aroused the slumbering visions of equality and messianic change that had stirred the English during the time of the civil war a century earlier.[14] When the French Revolution destroyed the old

---

14. These themes are developed by Thompson in *The Making of the English Working Class.*

order in 1789 and proclaimed the dawn of liberty, equality, and fraternity, many English working men and women saw in that revolution the confirmation of the messianic hopes of radical Christianity.

In the French Revolution the aristocracy that had ruled France since feudal times was overthrown. Political representation was extended to the Third Estate--the "people" who were not of noble birth. Positions in government, the army, the courts, and the church, which previously had been reserved for the sons of the nobility, were opened up for anyone with the talent to fill them. Peasants seized the land on many of the large estates belonging to the aristocracy and to the church. The prerogatives of the nobles were abolished. The power of the king was limited by an elected assembly. And the freedoms of speech, press, religion, and assembly were affirmed.

In the early stages of the revolution these changes were achieved with minimal bloodshed. Members of the aristocracy, persuaded by the philosophers of the equality and rights of man, joined the people in dismantling the old order. Eventually, of course, elements within the aristocracy did resist the change and, calling on the assistance of the monarchs of Europe, made war upon the French revolution. In time, the guillotine did its awful work on aristocrats and revolutionaries alike. And in time, it became clear that what the revolution had achieved was not the liberation of the "people" as a whole but rather the freedom of the bourgeoisie to crown their mastery of the economic life of the people with laws more suited to their ends. As early as June 1791, the elected assembly, which was dominated by spokesmen of the bourgeoisie, passed legislation outlawing labor unions. With the defeat of the Jacobins and the deliverance of power into more moderate hands, it became clear that the revolution no longer aimed at the emancipation of the people as a whole.

Two years after the overthrow of Maximilien Robespierre, members of the Society of Equals were arrested and charged with conspiracy to overthrow the government. The basic ideas of the group were set forth in the *Manifesto of the Equals*, written by Sylvain Marechal in April 1796. The *Manifesto* proclaimed that "the French Revolution is only the herald of another revolution, far greater, far more solemn, which will be the last of them all." And it made clear that the aim of this revolution was the real equality of all persons. "We are speaking of something more sublime and more equitable, the **Common Good** or the **Community of Goods**. No more individual ownership of the land: *the land belongs to no* *one*. We are demanding, we desire, communal enjoyment of the fruits of the earth; *the fruits belong to all*."[15] The leader of the conspiracy was François-Noël Babeuf, who had taken the name Gracchus of the Roman brothers who were tribunes of the poor. In the *Analysis of the Doctrine of Babeuf by the Babouvists* (1796), the charge of betrayal of the revolutionary hopes of the people is clear. "The Revolution is not finished, because the rich are absorbing all goods and are exclusively in command, while the poor are toiling in a state of virtual slavery; they languish in misery and are nothing in the State."[16] At his trial Babeuf was uncompromising:

> To reach a certain goal, one must vanquish everything that stands in the way. Now, as to the hypothesis of social change in question, whether one chooses to describe it, after the fashion of the plaintiffs, as subversive of the social order or to characterize it, in chorus with the philosophers and the great legislators, as a sublime regeneration, it is indubitable that this change could not be brought about except by the overthrow of the established government and the suppression of everything in the way.[17]

Babeuf was executed later that year. His example would inspire subsequent revolutionaries in France, as we shall see. For now the important point is that the rhetoric of liberty, equality, and fraternity could be seen from two perspectives. From the viewpoint of the bourgeoisie it meant the equal right of all male property holders to vote in elections, the liberty of each to express himself (however he could afford to do so), and the equal right of each to exchange his goods in free markets. For the working class liberty, equality, and fraternity meant the emancipation of every man from the domination of others, equality of material condition, and a community of equals.

In the early days of the revolution these differences were not so apparent. The revolution appeared as an unprecedented break in the continuity of history. It seemed to promise nothing less than the emancipation of humankind both from the rule of tyrants and from its own self-imposed slavery to custom, ignorance, and superstition. This vision of the universal emancipation of humankind had an intoxicating

---

15. Albert Fried and Ronald Sanders, eds., *Socialist Thought: A Documentary History* (Garden City: Anchor, 1964), pp. 52, 53.

16. Ibid., p. 56.

17. Ibid., p. 61.

effect on certain elements of the English working class and the English intelligentsia.[18]

In the 1790s a number of working-class organizations began to take shape in many of the industrial centers of England. Trade unions, though they were illegal until 1824, began to develop a group of competent leaders and took steps toward national organization. Friendly societies, in which workers joined together for social interaction and for the provision of insurance and burial benefits to members, spread and became infected with trade unionist and Jacobin ideas. In most of the major cities corresponding societies were formed in which members could discuss the latest news from France and debate the issues of the day. In spite of repressive legislation that included the banning of working-class organizations, censorship, arrests, the suspension of habeas corpus, imprisonment, exile, and execution, radical ideas continued to work their way throughout the working class.[19]

In the years following the French revolution England was, in the words of the historian A.J.P. Taylor, "the most disturbed country in civilized Europe."[20] Various segments of the working class, suffering extreme distress, seethed with a potent mixture of religion and political ideology. In 1817 there was a large hunger march on London that aimed at taking the city by storm.[21] In the early 1830s agricultural wage laborers began to destroy the threshing machines that were replacing

---

18. "Bliss was it in that dawn to be alive." This line from the *Prelude* by William Wordsworth expresses well the reception of the French revolution among some of the English romantic poets. On the importance of revolution to these poets, see M. H. Abrams, "English Romanticism," in Northrop Frye, ed., *Romanticism Reconsidered* (New York: Columbia University Press, 1963).

19. On the execution of Colonel Despard and other repressive measures of the time, see Thompson, *English Working Class*, p. 172. Of these times the poet William Blake said, "The Beast and the Whore rule without control." Ibid., p. 175.

20. A.J.P. Taylor, *Revolutions and Revolutionaries* (New York: Atheneum, 1980), p. 41. The explosive nature of social conditions in England in the early part of the nineteenth century is vividly conveyed in this passage from R. N. Salaman, *The History and Social Influence of the Potato*: "The use of the potato . . . did, in fact, enable the workers to survive on the lowest possible wages. It may be that in this way the potato prolonged and encouraged, for another hundred years, the impoverishment and degradation of the English masses; but what was the alternative, surely nothing but bloody revolution. That England escaped such a violent upheaval in the early decades of the nineteenth century . . . must in large measure be placed to the credit of the potato." Quoted in Thompson, *English Working Class*, p. 315.

21. Taylor, *Revolutions and Revolutionaries*, p. 41.

them. In putting down this uprising, the authorities hanged 9 laborers, sent 400 to prison, and sent another 450 into exile.[22]

Direct working-class challenge to the political rule of the rich came to a head in the Chartist movement. Because of property restrictions on the franchise, the vast majority of the working class was not eligible to vote in parliamentary elections. In 1819 a peaceful demonstration in Manchester in support of the right to vote was fired on by the police. Eleven people were killed and 500 injured. By the 1830s the right to vote became the focus of the People's Charter. The central demands of the Charter were for universal manhood suffrage, equally sized parliamentary districts, annual parliaments, vote by ballot, elimination of property requirements for becoming a member of parliament, and payment of members of parliament. Acceptance of the reforms would give the working class, which was the largest class, the power to pass whatever other reforms were needed to correct the economic distress of the English people. Lacking the vote, the Chartists adopted a strategy that called for the presentation of a petition with millions of signatures to parliament. In 1839 the petition was presented to parliament--which rejected it by a large majority.

In spite of revolutionary rhetoric and a minor armed insurrection led by the Chartist John Frost, delegates to a subsequent Chartist convention could not decide on any alternative course of action. Agitation for the Charter continued, and another major demonstration was held in the revolutionary year of 1848. But again, nothing came of it. In England much of the working class (and all women) remained excluded from the franchise throughout the remainder of the nineteenth century. Faced with the intransigence of parliament and unwilling to venture on armed insurrection, many of the leaders of the Chartist movement emigrated to the United States.

But there were a number of other efforts to improve life for working people. One scheme that grew out of the Chartist movement involved a plan to restore the working class to the land. Money was put up to buy large estates. Schools and other public buildings were built on these estates, and the remaining land was then divided into small plots. These plots were distributed by lot to individuals who were to farm them and pay rent to the Chartist fund, which would then buy more estates and continue the process.

In the 1820s and 1830s working-class struggle also turned to a number of experiments designed to extricate the working people from the capitalist system altogether. One such proposal involved the setting up

---

22. Ibid., pp. 43-44.

of labor exchanges. In the early part of the nineteenth century, much of the work was done in small shops or even in workers' homes. The control of the capitalist masters over their workers resided in the system of wage labor that left the masters in control of the products produced. Labor exchanges were countercultural institutions that, it was hoped, would provide working people with an alternative to wage labor and capitalist markets. Workers would bring objects they had produced to the labor exchange. The worker would receive credit equivalent to the amount of labor he or she spent in producing this object. This credit could then be used to purchase any other object of like labor value available in the labor exchange. The hope was that eventually, in this way, working people could trade directly with one another and avoid giving up profits to their capitalist masters.

During this period several experiments were also made with cooperatives. Consumers' cooperatives were set up to enable workers to buy needed staples at lower costs. Producers' cooperatives enabled workers to pool their assets in order to set up enterprises in which the full proceeds of the sale of the commodities produced returned to the producers themselves. And finally, attempts were also made to set up whole communities of associated producers who, it was hoped, would be able to arrange their economic life in such a way as to achieve plenty for each and escape the horrors of bondage to the capitalist system of production. A number of these communities were established, both in England and in the United States.

Thus by the middle of the nineteenth century a working-class movement had already established itself as part of the new world created by capitalism. Faced with desperate conditions, the working class experimented with various paths to liberation. Many of the ideas that were tried at that time--producers' cooperatives, labor exchanges, and utopian communities, for example--remain as recurring countercultural strategies for coping with the modern world. There is in this experimental groping a certain pragmatic open-mindedness. But it is also true that these experiments were understood within a cultural context established by the ideology of the Enlightenment. Science and industry had been revolutionized. And in the revolutions of seventeenth century England and eighteenth century France the political world had been revolutionized as well. Enlightenment, change, and progress were in the air. Working-class culture was a part of this broader cultural context. It aimed to apply reason to the task of emancipation. The socialist movement that spread in the second half of the nineteenth century offered the working-class movement an understanding of itself as part of this broader historical project of human emancipation. It is to this socialist movement that we now turn.

2

Christians, Communists, Anarchists, and Socialists

By the middle of the nineteenth century "the social question," which meant the problems of slums, poverty, pauperism, hunger, disease, drugs, crime, and prostitution, was beginning to emerge as an element in the popular consciousness of the middle classes. At the same time, at a more theoretical level, a number of diagnoses of these problems appeared that prescribed "socialism" as the answer to the social question. But different thinkers meant different things by "socialism"; and even where thinkers agreed as to what socialism was, there remained room for disagreement as to why it was necessary and how to achieve it.

The workers' movement grew out of the very practical distress experienced by a large part of the working class. The various theories of socialism that appeared in the nineteenth century were meant to address the problems of the working class, but they addressed these problems from a broader and more theoretical perspective.

Consider, for example, the socialist theory of Charles Fourier. As we saw in Chapter 1 the English workers' movement had been led to experiment with utopian communities. A similar strategy was adopted by Fourier. Fourier thought that the emerging system of industrial capitalism was unfit for human habitation. Where Adam Smith glorified the division of labor, Fourier saw in it a deadening monotony inconsistent with the love of variety inherent in human nature. In place of the capitalist system Fourier proposed a system of self-sufficient communities, which he called "phalansteries" (house of a phalanx, a group of people united in purpose). These phalansteries were to be inhabited by 810 men and 810 women, each selected to represent one of the various personality types identified by Fourier.

Within these phalansteries each person was free to do whatever he or she liked. Fourier thought that human beings had a natural need and love for productive labor and that, given the freedom to express their productive nature in their own way, each would experience productive labor itself as a form of play. There was to be no system of government within the phalanstery. Decisions were to be made by the inhabitants as a whole. Men and women were to have equal rights. Fourier was an ardent feminist who both recognized the oppression of women under capitalism and all previous societies and valued distinctly feminine qualities. The vision of Fourier was not the vision of a drab egalitarianism in which equality meant sameness. For him, not the melting pot but the salad bowl filled with different but complementary qualities was the proper metaphor for the good society. He devised a detailed architectural plan for the needed housing, living areas, and agricultural and industrial facilities. The family was to be abolished. Children were to be raised communally. Sexual relations were limited only by the principle that no harm was to be done to others. In general, Fourier maintained that the satisfaction of sexual and all other desires was not only necessary for psychic health but valuable in itself.[1]

This socialism of Fourier clearly includes a lot more than practical solutions to the problems of workers and their families. This proposal is typical of the socialist theories of his time. Socialism was seen as a radically different way of life. It addressed spiritual problems of alienation and unhappiness as well as material problems. Fourier's thoughts were interlaced with some very strange ideas (that with the coming of the socialism of phalansteries the sea would turn to lemonade, that stars have souls, and that the planets copulate, for example). But some of the themes that appear in his works--especially those regarding the goodness of human nature, the possibility of transforming work into play, the model of self-sufficient communities, feminism, and the exploration of alternatives to the nuclear family—have appeared over and over again in subsequent socialist theories and practice. This is not to say that all socialists have agreed with Fourier in these matters. Probably most have not. Nor is it to say that those who did embrace these ideas got them from Fourier. The point is just that "socialism" was commonly understood in a very broad sense as aiming at the total emancipation of all human beings from every form of oppression and dehumanization.

Fourier's ideas, however entangled with incredible fantasies they may have been, nonetheless touched on a number of deeply felt aspirations of human beings. In the nineteenth century there were over forty Fourierist

---

1.   On Fourier, see Leszek Kolakowski, *Main Currents of Marxism* , vol. 1 (Oxford: Oxford University Press, 1978), pp. 198-203 and Albert S. Lindemann, *A History of European Socialism* (New Haven: Yale University Press, 1983), pp. 38-42.

settlements in the United States.[2] Although no one of these even closely resembled the detailed plan for the phalansteries worked out by Fourier, each claimed to find some inspiration in his works, and men and women were found who were willing to put their fortunes and their lives into the dream of building socialist communities.

Typically, socialist theories confronted three tasks. First, they needed to explain the root causes of social problems. Second, they needed to offer some alternative vision of how human beings might live together in a way that would avoid the problems of the current system. Third, they needed to offer some strategy for how to realize the alternative social system. In the socialist theory of Fourier the root cause of social problems was the alleged poor fit between human nature and the demands of capitalism. The phalansteries were the proposed alternative way of life. And reasoned persuasion was the way to get there. Underlying all of this theory was Fouriers' playful and erotic vision of human nature.

Christian socialism offered a somewhat different view of human nature. Thus, for example, the Christian socialist Etienne Cabet blamed the problems of his age on human covetousness and greed. He preached an austere ethic of the renunciation of desire and diversity. His utopia was built on a foundation of strict equality--even in such basic matters as food, clothing, and shelter. He maintained that private property was the source of the evils suffered by the proletariat and urged the communal ownership of all property as the single necessary solution for these evils. In the Icarian communities envisaged by Cabet, each person had a duty to contribute whatever he or she could to the common good; and each was to receive whatever he or she needed, although the understanding of what was truly needed was marked by the austere egalitarianism mentioned above. And although the people as a whole were ultimately supposed to govern themselves, Cabet insisted on the duty of each to subordinate self to the good of the whole. No political parties were to be allowed and censorship was to control what people could read. Clearly there was quite a difference between the utopia of Cabet and the utopia of Fourier.

Underlying the socialism of Cabet was an appeal to the teachings of Christianity. After all, did not Christ tell the rich young man to give

---

2. Mark Holloway, *Heavens on Earth* (New York: Liberty, 1951), p. 141. Probably the most famous of these settlements was Brook Farm, which began as a Fourierist phalanstery and then deliberately rejected this identification in favor of an identity of its own making.

away all that he had to the poor?[3] And does not scripture tell us that the disciples of Christ practiced communism?

> Now the company of those who believed were of one heart and soul, and no one said that any of the things which he possessed was his own, but they had everything in common. . . . There was not a needy person among them, for as many as were possessors of lands or houses sold them, and brought the proceeds of what was sold and laid it at the apostles' feet; and distribution was made to each as any had need.[4]

Here scripture could be construed as offering a clear endorsement of communism: the common ownership of goods. But how to reach this communism was an issue over which Christian socialists were deeply divided. Some, like Cabet, favored the establishment of self-sufficient Christian communities by means of moral persuasion. Others, like the German tailor Wilhelm Weitling, advocated the revolutionary and, if need be, violent seizure of state power and the establishment of Christian communism on a national basis.[5] Here we see that similar philosophical foundations, in this case Christian ethics, gave rise to very different conceptions of the socialist goal and very different conceptions of the way to reach that goal.

Another powerful current in nineteenth century socialist thought was provided by the natural rights theory of John Locke, which played an important role in the American and French revolutions. In order to understand how socialists appealed to the principles of Locke, we must first take a brief look at the economics of Adam Smith. Here we will discover ideas that would also play a role in the socialism of Marx and Engels.

In the classical economics of Adam Smith there are several distinct theories of value suggested at different places in the text. One of these theories is the labor theory of value. In a simplified version, the labor theory stated that the value of commodities is proportional to the labor time necessary to produce them.[6] Smith went on to say that in early

---

3.   Mark 10:17-25.

4.   Acts 4:32-35.

5.   On Cabet see Kolakowski, *Main Currents*, pp. 213-214, and Lindemann, *European Socialism*, pp. 68-69. On the fate of Icarian communities based on Cabet's teachings in the United States, see Holloway, *Heavens on Earth*. On Weitling, see Kolakowski, *Main Currents*, pp. 211-213, and Lindemann, *European Socialism*, pp. 77-78.

6.   "In that early and rude state of society which precedes both the accumulation of stock and the appropriation of land, the proportion between the quantities of labour necessary for acquiring different objects seems to be the only circumstance which can

times, before the land became the private property of some people and before production came under the mastery of the capitalist, all of what was produced belonged to the laborer. "In that original state of things, which precedes both the appropriation of land and the accumulation of stock, the whole produce of labour belongs to the labourer. He has neither landlord nor master to share with him."[7] But "as soon as land becomes private property, the landlord demands a share of almost all the produce which the labourer can either raise, or collect from it. His rent makes the first deduction from the produce of the labour which is employed upon the land."[8] And of course, the capitalist also demands a deduction from the produce of the laborer as payment for the use of his capital. "This profit makes a second deduction from the produce of the labour which is employed upon land."[9] In *The Principles of Political Economy* (1817), David Ricardo, Smith's great successor, eliminated many of the contradictions in Smith's work and developed a powerful theoretical economics constructed around the labor theory of value. Like Smith, Ricardo viewed labor as the source of value, labor time as its measure, and profit and rent as deductions from the produce of labor.[10]

In the 1820s a number of English champions of the cause of the working class used the labor theory of value of Smith and Ricardo to develop an argument, contrary to the spirit of Smith and Ricardo, against the morality of capitalism. The argument had two premises. The first of these is the labor theory of value itself--labor is the source of all value. The second premise, one which Marx and Engels would reject, is the principle of property rights advanced by the philosopher John Locke--that every person has a right to the produce of his own labor.[11] From these two principles it follows that workers, who produce all value, have a right to own all that is produced. Since, under capitalism, the product

---

afford any rule for exchanging them for one another. If among a nation of hunters, for example, it usually costs twice the labour to kill a beaver which it does to kill a deer, one beaver should naturally exchange for or be worth two deer. It is natural that what is usually the produce of two days' or two hours' labour, should be worth double of what is usually the produce of one day's or one hour's labour." Adam Smith, *An Inquiry into the Nature and Causes of the Wealth of Nations* (1776) (New York: Modern Library, 1937), p. 47.

7.   Ibid., p. 64.

8.   Ibid., p. 65.

9.   Ibid., p. 65.

10.   David Ricardo, *The Principles of Political Economy (1817)*, chap. 1, sec. 1 (London: Everyman, 1962), pp. 6-7.

11.   John Locke, *Second Treatise of Civil Government*, chap. 5, sec. 27, in John Locke, *Two Treatises of Government* (1690) (Cambridge: Cambridge University Press, 1963), pp. 328-329.

of labor is appropriated by the capitalist, capitalism violates workers' rights.[12]

An important variant of this natural rights socialism was offered in the anarchist philosophy of Pierre Joseph Proudhon, who would later quarrel with Marx over the leadership of the socialist movement. At the center of his thought was the natural right of liberty of every individual. Like the Ricardian socialists, Proudhon rejected all forms of unearned income, such as rent and profit, as immoral deductions coercively extracted from the real producers. "Property is theft," said Proudhon. In place of capitalism and private property he advocated a decentralized system of producers' cooperatives in which workers would join together on a purely voluntary basis. These workers' cooperatives would enter into voluntary cooperation and exchange with other workers' cooperatives in accordance with the principle of mutuality, which provided that all parties should mutually benefit from cooperation. His strong anarchist opposition to any form of coercion also led Proudhon to reject revolutionary violence and trade unionist strikes as legitimate means of working-class struggle. He even rejected electoral politics as a path to the cooperative society of the future, since voting as to who should rule implicitly involves approval of the principle of the coercive rule of the state itself.[13]

Ferdinand Lassalle, who had no scruples about coercive force, agreed with the anarchist Proudhon in his vision of socialism as a system of worker-owned and worker-managed producers' cooperatives. He tried to persuade the Prussian government to provide funds for the formation of producers' cooperatives in which the value produced would accrue entirely to the workers who produced it.[14] Thus we see it was also possible for socialists with widely differing philosophical foundations to reach similar conclusions about the desired form of the socialist society of the future. For although Lassalle agreed with Proudhon in advocating

---

12. Among those who advanced this argument were Thomas Hodgskin, William Thompson, Francis Bray, and John Gray. On these "Ricardian Socialists," see Maurice Dobb, *Theories of Value and Distribution Since Adam Smith* (Cambridge: Cambridge University Press, 1973), pp. 137-141.

13. On Proudhon, see Lindemann, *European Socialism*, pp. 106-109, and Kolakowski, *Main Currents*, pp. 203-211. Kolakowski rightly emphasizes Proudhon's inconsistency on a number of issues (he glorified war, which is certainly coercive, and appears to have accepted male rule over women as just).

14. On Lassalle, see Kolakowski, *Main Currents*, pp. 238-244, and Lindemann, *European Socialism*, pp. 102-104. Lindemann's account leaves out the idea of producers' cooperatives and in this way overlooks one of the fundamental differences between Lassalle and Marx.

a system of producers' cooperatives, he did not share Proudhon's anarchist rejection of the coercive state.

The socialist theories sketched above provide but a sample of the different socialisms offered up in the nineteenth century. What they all have in common is a sense that something was deeply wrong with the newly formed capitalist order and a sense that some alternative way of life had to be found to replace it. By the 1840s many of these socialist ideas were circulating throughout Europe.

There was considerable unevenness in the extent of the development of capitalism in the various European countries. England was certainly the most advanced capitalist country. But capitalism was also well developed in countries like Holland and France, and capitalist institutions were significantly present throughout Western Europe. In England, Holland, and France the bourgeoisie was firmly in control. In other countries, like Prussia, the bourgeoisie was still excluded from political power. The "social question" was more or less prominent in people's minds, depending on the extent of capitalist development in the country of their experience.

"Socialism" at this time was not some clearly defined economic or political doctrine. Rather it was a soup of the different, and often inconsistent, ideas discussed above. For some "socialism" meant welfare state capitalism. For others it meant producers' cooperatives, cooperative communities, or egalitarian states. For some it meant all these things at once, in a kind of jumbled and confused picture, where the incoherencies went unnoticed, clouded by the passionate hope and expectation of a better world to come. For some "socialism" was associated with progress, higher ideals, human kindness, and emancipation. For others "socialism" conjured up visions of revolutionary destruction, bloodshed, repression, and meanness of spirit. "Socialism" was not distinguished from "communism."[15] And both of these terms were sometimes confused with "republican," perhaps on the assumption that if the "republican" demand for the right to vote were granted to the working class, socialism would surely be the outcome.

In many quarters it was still believed that the French revolutionary marriage of the bourgeoisie and the proletariat could be salvaged. If only employers and workers would cooperate and work together, the social problems of the times could be overcome. In other quarters the

---

15. Lindemann, *European Socialism*, p. 50, claims that "socialism" was usually linked with the principle "to each according to work" and "communism" with the principle "to each according to need." But he admits that this usage was not consistently adhered to.

"social question" had not even entered consciousness, and the central issues of the day were cast in terms of the earlier contest between "the people" and the aristocracy.

One simple but powerful current within nineteenth century socialist thought represented a continuation of the outlook of Gracchus Babeuf. According to this viewpoint, it was apparent that the rich remained in control and that the working poor had little to show for the successful overthrow of the feudal aristocracy. What was needed was another revolution to overthrow the rich. Let those who understand band together. Let them wait for the right moment. Then let them overthrow the government by force and establish in its place a dictatorship that would rule on behalf of the people as a whole. The chief representative of this outlook in the history of nineteenth-century socialism is Louis-Auguste Blanqui. A historian of modern socialism gave this sketch of Blanqui's life:

> He became acquainted with various socialist doctrines that were going about, and took an active part in the July Revolution [in France in 1830]. In the thirties he organized clandestine societies of a radical-democratic nature, inclining more and more to socialism. He was put on trial in January 1832 and made a celebrated speech of accusation rather than defence, proclaiming the just war of the proletariat against the rich and the oppressor. He was imprisoned for a year, after which he resumed conspiratorial activity and led an unsuccessful revolt against the monarchy in May 1839. Sentence of death was passed, but commuted to life imprisonment. Liberated by the 1848 Revolution, he became one of the chief leaders of the Paris working class, but was soon behind bars again. He was released in 1859 for a brief period, but spent most of the sixties in gaol. Under Thiers's regime, he was released, and again arrested in March 1871; he was elected *in absentia* to the leadership of the Paris Commune, in whose ranks his followers were the most active and resolute faction. He remained in prison till 1879, and thereafter continued to agitate for the remaining two years of his life.[16]

Blanqui spent over forty years of his adult life in prison. Alexis de Tocqueville, who saw Blanqui during one of his brief periods out of prison, described him in this way: "He seemed to have passed his life in a sewer and to have just left it. . . . He had sunken, wrinkled cheeks and white lips. . . . His clothes seemed to be covered with mold; no evidence

---

16. Kolakowski, *Main Currents*, p. 215.

of underclothing. A black cloak covered his thin and meagre members."[17]

As a theoretician of socialism, Blanqui did not have much to offer. If pressed as to what a socialist society would be like, his only answer was that it was first necessary to make the revolution.[18] He thought that exploitation and poverty were the result of unequal exchanges in which workers received less than full value for their labor power, but he lacked any theory of value or explanation for why such unequal exchanges persisted. He was distrustful of the Chartist solution of universal manhood suffrage, thinking that the majority was ignorant and easily misled. Instead of democracy he favored the dictatorship of a revolutionary group committed to the cause of the poor. His efforts were entirely focused on the task of achieving a successful rising, which he thought could be done by a select group of well-organized revolutionaries.

It is this conception of the revolutionary process as the action of a heroic conspiratorial elite that became known as Blanquism in subsequent years. With few exceptions this conception of the revolutionary process was rejected by other socialists. When, later, Lenin called for a small disciplined party of full-time revolutionaries committed to the cause of establishing a dictatorship of the proletariat, most socialists denounced Lenin for his "Blanquist" tendencies. What Blanqui left to the socialist tradition was not a great body of thought concerning either the socialist future or the revolutionary process but rather an example of revolutionary commitment and courage. Marx was no admirer of Blanqui the thinker, but in his account of the revolutionary rising of the Paris Commune in 1871, he pays tribute to Blanqui. "The Commune again and again had offered to exchange the archbishop, and ever so many priests in the bargain, against the single Blanqui, then in the hands of Thiers. Thiers obstinately refused. He knew that with Blanqui he would give to the Commune a head."[19]

The decade of the 1840s opened with the publication of major works by Cabet, Louis Blanc, Weitling, and Proudhon and with an attempted revolutionary insurrection by Blanqui. In 1847 European capitalism experienced a depression that simultaneously affected those countries in which capitalism was significantly developed. Mass unemployment was common. There was no system of unemployment compensation or other

17. Lindemann, *European Socialism*, p. 72.
18. A.J.P. Taylor, *Revolutions and Revolutionaries* (New York: Atheneum, 1980), p. 70.
19. Karl Marx, *The Civil War in France* (1870) (Moscow: Progress, 1974), p. 75.

governmental apparatus for responding to the crisis. Without the right
to vote the European working class was almost driven to revolutionary
insurrection. Riots occurred. In England the People's Charter was
revived, and a tense Chartist meeting occurred on Kennington Common
in April 1848. Troops under the command of the Duke of Wellington
were called out to intimidate the Chartists and guarantee there would be
no rioting. The peaceful petition for the right to vote again met with
rejection by Parliament.

In France, in February 1848, revolutionary agitation succeeded in
forcing Louis Philippe to abdicate the throne. A republic was
proclaimed, based on the principle of universal manhood suffrage.
Inspired by the French example, within that incredible year,
revolutionary movements swept nearly all of the countries of Europe. It
would be wrong to view these revolutionary risings as "socialist." The
revolutionary movements of 1848 arose from the confluence of various
forces. In those countries in which unlimited monarchy and aristocratic
privilege continued to rule, the revolutionary movement was often
primarily a matter of "the people" attempting to overthrow the
aristocracy and win the institutions of representative government. And
in Germany and Italy, the cause of national unification, which had to
overcome the political structures of the existing local aristocracies, was a
powerful force for revolutionary change. But in every country, even
where these other issues dominated the course of events, the particular
interests of the working class played a part in the overall revolutionary
process. Workers joined the revolutionary struggle in hopes of finding
some redress for their problems. Their concentration in key cities made
them a valuable asset for the revolutionary cause. It is also true that their
presence in the revolutionary struggle disturbed their bourgeois allies.
In a sense the social question, and the prospect of revolutionary
communism, haunted the revolutions of 1848. The bourgeoisie could not
win without the workers, but in the end it feared them more than it
wanted to free itself from the monarchy and the aristocracy. In her study
of the revolutions of 1848, Priscilla Robertson observed that "in a sense,
the 1848 revolutions turned into class struggles, and failed because they
did."[20]

This transformation of a broader revolutionary opposition against
monarchy into class war is most clearly shown in the experience of
France in 1848. After the February revolution the poet, Alphonse

---

20. Priscilla Robertson, *Revolutions of 1848: A Social History* (Princeton: Princeton
University Press, 1971), p. 412.

Lamartine, a member of the provisional government formed at that time, proclaimed that the revolution had "eliminated the terrible misunderstanding . . . between the classes."[21] But as the weeks passed tensions between the classes increased. Armed groups of workers under the leadership of Blanqui marched to the government headquarters where they sullenly listened to the promises of their "socialist" minister Louis Blanc. In the campaign for the elections that were to establish a regular government, preservation of law and order became an increasingly common campaign promise. In May Blanqui led a band of armed workers who dispersed the National Assembly, declared it dissolved, and announced the formation of a new provisional government. This uprising was put down by force.

Louis Blanc, a socialist member of the provisional government, had attempted to meet the needs of the unemployed workers of Paris by instituting a system of national workshops, which provided public employment for the unemployed. This costly system was unpopular with the bourgeoisie and with the masses of family farmers in the countryside who paid the bill. In June conservative opposition to the national workshops prevailed. Unmarried men were expelled from the workshops altogether, and married men were ordered to leave Paris for work in the provinces. Unorganized revolt broke out in the working-class districts of Paris. Barricades were erected in all of the poorer districts. The government responded with force, and class war erupted in the streets of Paris. In the end the government prevailed, but only by recourse to violent repression. De Tocqueville called the conflict "the greatest slave war in modern times."[22] Between June 24 and June 28 more people were killed than in the entire period of the French Revolution. The June days in France provided sobering food for thought.[23]

In the *Manifesto of the Communist Party*, which appeared in 1848, Karl Marx and Frederick Engels offered yet another version of socialism to nineteenth-century readers. In this work they tried to distinguish their own version of socialism from the various alternative socialisms that surrounded them. In doing so, they laid the foundations for the version of socialism from which communism would be derived. Having gained some sense of the milieu within which their ideas developed, we will

---

21. Quoted in Lindemann, *European Socialism*, p. 81.
22. Quoted in Taylor, *Revolutions and Revolutionaries*, p. 80.
23. Ibid., p. 80. Taylor claims that 15,000 were killed during the June days themselves "and many more afterwards." He also claims that 20,000 were sent to penal settlements overseas.

now try to give some understanding of the specifically Marxist branch of the socialist tree that would eventually lead to communism. But it is also important to keep in mind that Marxism was only a single voice in the (somewhat cacophonous) socialist choir. Like the other socialist theories of its day, it was a response to both the problems and the aspirations of its time. In assessing the significance of the fall of communism, we need to consider not only Marxism but also the broader socialist movement of which it was a part.

3

The Scientific Socialism
of Marx and Engels

Early in February 1848, a few weeks before the overthrow of the monarchy in France, Karl Marx and Frederick Engels sent to the printer in London the German text of their just completed *Manifesto of the Communist Party*. Written as a platform for the Communist League, a largely German revolutionary organization, the *Manifesto* has become a classic statement of the scientific socialism of Marx and Engels. In it Marx and Engels sketched a theory of capitalism (which would later be more fully developed in Marx's *Capital*); outlined their theory of historical materialism, which attempts to chart and explain the course of historical development; differentiated their own conception of socialism from the various alternative conceptions of socialism current in the mid-nineteenth century; and offered suggestions to guide the struggle for the emancipation of the working class.

Marx and Engels saw capitalism as an enormously successful engine for the production of wealth. In the *Manifesto*, they praised the capitalists for their unprecedented development of the productive powers of humankind: "The bourgeoisie, during its rule of scarce one hundred years, has created more massive and more colossal productive forces than have all preceding generations together."[1] In place of the traditional ways of life that had been followed, more or less unchanged, throughout the roughly 1,000 years of European feudalism, capitalism substituted a dynamic, ever-changing way of life. In place of superstition, prejudice, and narrow-minded nationalism, capitalism fostered science, open-mindedness, and internationalism.

---

1. Karl Marx and Frederick Engels, *Manifesto of the Communist Party* (1848) (Progress: Moscow, 1977), p. 48.

29

All fixed, fast-frozen relations, with their train of ancient and venerable prejudices and opinions, are swept away, all new-formed ones become antiquated before they can ossify. All that is solid melts into air, all that is holy is profaned, and man is at last compelled to face with sober senses, his real conditions of life, and his relations with his kind. . . .[2] In place of the old local and national seclusion and self-sufficiency, we have intercourse in every direction, universal inter-dependence of nations. And as in material, so also in intellectual production. The intellectual creations of individual nations become common property. National one-sidedness and narrow-mindedness become more and more impossible, and from the numerous national and local literatures, there arises a world literature.[3]

In his major scientific work, *Capital* (published in 1867), Marx developed a theoretical understanding of these dynamic properties of capitalist systems of production.[4] At the heart of capitalism is a compelling drive toward the accumulation of capital. For a capitalist firm, long-term profitability is necessary for survival. Each firm is in constant competition with its rivals for its share of the market. Faced with the unremitting pressure of competition, each capitalist is motivated to produce as efficiently as possible. In an effort to reduce per unit costs of production and expand its share of the market, each capitalist firm is motivated to adopt innovative techniques of production. Bigger operations bring economies of scale. New, capital-intensive technologies reduce per unit costs of production. The innovative firm is able to produce more for less, thereby to undercut its rivals, increase its share of the market, drive its competitors out of the market, raise its rate of profit, and survive. Competing firms must either adopt the new techniques, or some yet more productive technology, or go under. In the periodic recessions in the business cycle the larger more successful firms survive and devour their smaller rivals.

Faced with such a competitive environment, all capitalists are motivated to increase their capital in order to survive. Since each capitalist is motivated in this way, capitalism brings with it a systematic tendency for the accumulation of capital goods--the mines, machines, factories, farms, and means of communication, transport, and

---

2.   Ibid., p. 46.

3.   Ibid., p. 47.

4.   See especially chapter 24, section 3, "Separation of Surplus-Value Into Capital and Revenue: The Abstinence Theory," and chapter 25, "The General Law of Capitalist Accumulation," in Karl Marx, *Capital* (1867), vol. 1 (New York: International, 1973), pp. 591-598, 612-707.

coordination that make their productive use possible. The capitalist system yokes the self-interested behavior of each individual capitalist to the task of building up the productive capacities of humankind as a whole.

So far, Marx's analysis follows along lines developed by Adam Smith. Like Smith, Marx appreciated the dynamic creativity of capitalism, and like Smith, Marx traced this dynamic creativity to the way in which capitalist systems provide incentives to each individual capitalist to produce more for less. But where Smith looked optimistically forward to a capitalist future of steady growth and increasing shares for all, Marx thought the development of capitalism, and its concomitant development of human productive powers, paradoxically brings with it the impoverishment of human life.

Briefly put, Marx argued that capitalism requires the sacrifice of human beings to the cause of the accumulation of capital. Driven to accumulate in order to survive, the capitalist is forced to exploit his workers as much as possible. Low wages and long hours mean higher profits. Higher profits mean survival. The capitalist who is too "soft" is driven from the field of competition. Smith's optimistic belief that capitalist accumulation would result in greater wealth for every person rested on the mistaken assumption that total outlays by the capitalist reappeared as wage income. Instead, Marx argued, capitalist accumulation resulted in ever-increasing "savings" instead of consumption.[5] Within a capitalist system production for human needs takes place only if such production is profitable--only if it serves the purpose of capital accumulation.

Further, as a capitalist system develops over time, capital is concentrated and centralized in fewer and fewer hands. In the sea of competition the big fish swallow the little fish. The small capitalists are driven from the field and join the ranks of wage laborers, the proletariat. Eventually competition itself gives way to oligopoly (the control of the market by a few firms) or monopoly (the control of the market by a single firm). Most people are stripped of their property. Having nothing to sell but their labor power, they become wage workers, forced to sell their labor power in order to survive. The supply of wage laborers is increased. And with the accumulation of capital fewer and fewer workers are needed to produce the goods consumed by society as a whole. The demand for wage laborers is reduced. The result is the creation of the industrial reserve army of unemployed laborers that

---

5.   On this point see ibid., pp. 588-591.

serves to keep wages down and that appears as an ever-increasing welfare burden on the capitalist economy.[6] Capitalism, which creates an unprecedented capacity for the production of wealth, condemns the masses of working people to a dreary life of long and arduous labor for the sake of the accumulation of yet more capital.

It is important to see that Marx does not blame the capitalist for this outcome. The capitalist does not intend the impoverishment of the lives of his workers: the "system" produces this effect. If the capitalist acts like the miser, bent on accumulating more and more wealth, in the capitalist this drive to accumulate is "the effect of the social mechanism, of which he is but one of the wheels."[7] Capitalism is "like the sorcerer, who is no longer able to control the powers of the nether world whom he has called up by his spells."[8]

Like the monster created by Dr. Frankenstein, capitalism turns on its creators. Capitalism is a system created by human beings in the course of their historical development. As a philosopher, Marx had meditated on human freedom. He had noted that, unlike other animals that reproduce the way of life of their ancestors unchanged, human beings are free from the dominance of instinct, able to change their way of life. It is this fundamental human capacity that makes us creatures capable of having a history. Human history is the record of human freedom acting within the constraints imposed by the past. Each generation receives from its ancestors a way of social life that it modifies and develops according to its own needs and discoveries. Capitalism is a humanly created way of life. Of course, this is not to say that anyone ever planned to create capitalism. In Marx's account capitalism emerged from the pores of feudal society as the unintended outcome of diverse individual actions in response to diverse economic, political, and cultural forces.[9] But the fact of history, the fact that human beings have transformed their interaction with nature and their way of life, points to a capacity of human beings that distinguishes them from other animals.

Heretofore, this capacity of human beings has not been fully developed. Here and there individuals have attempted to guide the course of history. But for the most part historical development has been unintended. And where individuals have tried to bend history to their will, the outcome, largely determined by misunderstood historical forces,

---

6.   Ibid., pp. 628-640.

7.   Ibid., p. 592.

8.   Marx and Engels, *Manifesto*, p. 49.

9.   For Marx's account of the origins of capitalism, see *Capital*, vol. 1, part 8, "The So-Called Primitive Accumulation," pp. 713-774.

has, more often than not, been far different from the intended effect. Under capitalism market forces rather than human deliberation guide the course of development. Each individual can react only to the market, and there is no institutional structure by which human beings could collectively master the forces of the market. Never before fully developed, under capitalism the human capacity for free historical action is completely alienated.[10]

This conception of human beings as having a capacity for creative historical action is fundamental to Marx's view of history. But to understand Marx's view of history, it is also necessary to understand the philosophy of history of Hegel against which Marx's own "materialist conception of history" was developed.

Hegel held a deeply spiritual view of reality. He thought that, at bottom, all of reality was spiritual in nature. Hegel was not religious in any traditional sense of the term. He did not, for example, believe in a creator God who had made the material universe. For him, there was not a material universe distinct from a realm of spiritual beings. For him, all of reality was spiritual and divine. What was ultimately real was the one conscious, creative, world Spirit. Every material thing, and every conscious human being, were but a small part of this ultimately real world Spirit.

Hegel thought of this Spirit as propelled by a quest for self-knowledge. Guided by demands of its own inner reason, the world Spirit gradually works out an ever-more-adequate conception of itself. History is the record of this voyage in self-understanding. Hegel thought of each form of human existence, each historically developed way of life, as exhibiting or reflecting a particular idea reached by the world Spirit in its quest for adequate self knowledge. As the world Spirit comes to see the limitations of one idea and goes on to develop a more adequate conception of itself, this change is reflected in human history in a qualitative transformation of the way of human life. In this sense, then, Hegel saw mundane human history as a reflection of divine history. There was, behind or beneath the accounts of the historians of human affairs, a deeper, philosophical history that explained the real meaning of human history. Every historical epoch was the realization of some

---

10. The term "alienation" has it roots in legal theory where to alienate a thing is to sell, give, or bequeath it to another. Inalienable rights are rights that cannot be given away. Under capitalism human nature is alienated in the sense that the human capacity for deliberate historical action aimed at the rational direction of social development is relinquished to blind market forces.

philosophical idea. The course of historical development was guided by the needs of philosophical rationality.

Marx rejected this Hegelian philosophy of history. For him, reality was not fundamentally spiritual. Marx was a materialist. He believe that the spiritual powers of human beings, their capacity for creative conscious life, gradually evolved from a nonconscious, nonspiritual, material universe. For Marx, there was no philosophical history that underlay mundane history. For him, historical change could not be explained in terms of the realization of philosophical ideas.

Where Hegel had put the philosophical development of the world Spirit, Marx put the economic development of humankind's powers of production at the foundation of his theory of history. Marx thought of the economic problem, the production of the goods necessary to sustain human existence, as the central problem facing humankind up to the present. Marx thought of each distinct historical form of human existence as a way of life organized around a particular solution to the economic problem. In each historical epoch humankind has available certain natural resources, a certain technology for the utilization of those resources, and a certain organizational capacity for applying the existing technology to the available resources. Together resources, technology, and organizational capacities constitute what Marx called the "forces of production."

In putting these forces of production to use, each historical epoch develops certain "relations of production." These relations of production are social relations between human beings that define the roles human beings fill in the course of producing the goods necessary for human survival. In some primitive societies these relations of production involve cooperation among equals. But in most societies the relations of production define distinct roles for distinct social classes. And these distinct roles involve relations of power and domination between members of one social class and members of another. Thus, for example, the economies of ancient Egypt, Greece, and Rome were dominated by the relation of production of master to slave. Marx argued that in contrast to this system, feudalism was dominated by the relation of production of lord to serf, and capitalism is dominated by the relation of production of capitalist to wage laborer.

The forces and relations of production together constituted what Marx called the economic base of the social system. Political institutions and legal systems formed parts of the ideological superstructure that would be built up around the economic base in response to the needs of the system of production. Thus, for example, in a feudal system in which each manor is largely self-sufficient, economic contracts were rare, and consequently no elaborate system of contract law was required. But in a capitalist system, where everyone is dependent on everyone else, an elaborate system of contract law would be required. Marx also saw morality, religion, art, and philosophy as parts of the ideological superstructure. Unlike Hegel, who saw morality and religion as expressions of the distinctive philosophical idea of the age, Marx saw morality and religion as ideologies, designed to legitimate and sanctify the relations of power and domination built into the economic foundation of the social system.

Unlike Hegel, who saw historical development as a reflection of philosophical development, Marx conceived of historical change as the result of the growth and development of the forces of production:

> At a certain stage of development, the material productive forces of society come into conflict with the existing relations of production or--this merely expresses the same thing in legal terms--with the property relations within the framework of which they have operated hitherto. From forms of development of the productive forces these relations turn into their fetters.[11]

When the productive forces outgrow the relations of production, society enters a period of revolutionary transformation. In such a period the class roles defined by the hitherto prevailing relations of production are called into question. The period of revolutionary transformation of the economic base is a period of intense class struggle. Eventually, Marx believed, there would emerge out of this class struggle new relations of production that would better facilitate further development of the forces of production and that would also define new class roles. And in consequence of this transformation of the economic base, the ideological superstructure would rapidly change to fit the new relations of production. Thus, following the bourgeois revolutions of the seventeenth, eighteenth, and nineteenth centuries, new legal systems arose to serve the needs of the emerging capitalist order, and in ethics the

---

11. Karl Marx, preface to *A Contribution to the Critique of Political Economy* (1859) (New York: International, 1972), p. 21. This passage and similar passages in other of Marx's works have suggested the view that economic factors determined the course of history and that ultimately changes in the economic sphere are determined by changes in technology. But other passages in Marx's works are difficult to reconcile with either an economic determinist or a technological determinist view of history. For a discussion of this point see Richard Miller, *Analyzing Marx*, part 3, "History" (Princeton: Princeton University Press, 1984).

theories of utilitarianism and natural rights, which supported this new order, vanquished the previously ascendent theories of the divine right of kings and the duties of passive obedience.

In this scheme of things what distinguishes one historical epoch from another is the distinct relations of production that dominate in each period. Marx thought it was possible to identify five fundamental historical epochs: primitive communism, ancient slave societies, feudalism, capitalism, and socialism. These epochs were sequentially ordered, each emerging from its predecessor and in turn giving birth to its successor. The whole process was viewed by Marx as a process of natural evolution. This was true in two ways. First, as a materialist Marx rejected any supernatural processes. Second, Marx saw the historical process as like a "natural" process in that it had not been subject to deliberate, rational, human control. One reason for this absence of rational control was that the determining forces of historical change--development of the productive forces, relations of production, classes and class struggle--were not understood. Another reason was that from the end of primitive communism to the dawn of socialism human social existence was marked by the struggle between social classes. At bottom the social order was an oppressive order. Not reason and deliberation but force and violence governed human affairs. Following the dawn of socialism and the creation of a classless society, for the first time the historical development of human social existence would come under the democratic, deliberate, rational control of human beings. In a sense, then, with the dawn of socialism history as "natural" evolution gives way to history as a deliberate human creation.[12]

This "materialist conception of history," as Marx and Engels were wont to call it, or "historical materialism" as it has come to be known in contemporary Marxist philosophy, has been seen by many as the central theoretical contribution of Marxism. But it is important to remember that this theory of history was only sketched by Marx. The most clearly developed statement of it comes in a mere two pages in the preface to *A Contribution to the Critique of Political Economy* (1859).[13] And elsewhere Marx denied that he had any general theory of history or that he had

---

12. Of course, even before socialism history is a human creation, but it is an unintended and irrational creation. And of course, even after socialism human beings remain "natural" in the sense opposed to "supernatural."

13. There is an extended discussion of history in the section of Karl Marx's and Frederick Engels's *The German Ideology* (1845) (New York: International, 1966) on "Feuerbach" but the categories of forces and relations of production are not rigorously developed there.

ever claimed to have discovered a general law of historical development that every society must follow. Instead of a "historico-philosophic theory of the general path every people is fated to tread," Marx called his historical work only a "sketch of the genesis of capitalism in Western Europe."[14] The real aim of Marx's philosophy of history is not to lay down laws of historical development or rigid categories for historical analysis but to dispel the Hegelian illusion of an esoteric philosophical history underlying the real history of humankind.

Nevertheless, Marx's historical "sketch" is sufficiently drawn to inform his political strategy. Like their fellow "socialists" of the mid-nineteenth century, Marx and Engels were appalled at the conditions of the working class. Like their fellow socialists, they saw in the new way of life created by capitalism a morally repugnant impoverishment of the human spirit. Like their fellow socialists, they decried the degeneration of social life to relations of greed and mutual use. Where they differed from their fellow socialists was in their understanding of what could be done about these conditions. The solution envisaged by Marx and Engels is informed by their sketch of the historical development of Western Europe. Roughly put, Marx aimed at fully utilizing the increased forces of production by replacing capitalist relations of production with socialist relations of production that would allow for the unfettered growth of the productive forces and that would eliminate the "contradictory" nature of capitalism within which growth of productive forces existed alongside constriction of the human spirit and dehumanization of the masses of working people.

Marx and Engels contrasted this historically informed vision of socialism with the alternative socialisms of their time. Thus for example, although they shared much of the moral outrage of Thomas Carlyle, they rejected his "feudal socialism" as an unrealistically romanticized view of the feudal past and as a hopeless effort to turn back the hands of time. Once modern forces of production had been set loose in the world, it was absurd to think humankind could return to the old ways or would want to abandon the potentially liberating productive powers created by capitalism. And similarly, the moral and spiritual aristocracy called for by Carlyle to lead England out of its spiritual decline was, so long as capitalist relations of production remained, doomed to ineffectualness.

---

14. See Marx's letter to the editorial board of *Otechestvenniye Zapiski* in Lewis Feuer, ed. *Marx and Engels: Basic Writings on Politics and Philosophy* (Garden City: Anchor, 1959), pp. 439-441.

Similarly, the "true socialism" of Karl Grün and others in Germany sought to overcome class conflict and realize a "true socialist society." But the true socialist society that was envisaged was in reality, according to Marx and Engels, only a sentimental and moralized version of precapitalist conditions in Germany. The German true socialists were thus, like the followers of Carlyle, swimming against the historical current of the time (and wearing rose-tinted goggles as well).

Likewise, Marx and Engels saw the petty-bourgeois socialism of Jean Sismondi, who attempted to preserve a society of small producers within a system of competitive markets and free trade, as doomed to failure. Such a system was bound to destroy itself as the competitive forces of the market fostered the very growth, concentration, and centralization of capital the petty-bourgeois socialists rejected.[15]

Marx and Engels made a related but somewhat different argument against the utopian socialisms of Fourier, Cabet, and Robert Owen. Unlike the reactionary and petty-bourgeois socialists, these socialists recognized the need for radically new forms of social organization. They proposed the establishment of model communities in which capitalist relations would be replaced by cooperative relations of production. Such proposals suffer two fundamental weaknesses. First, such "pocket editions of the New Jerusalem" cannot take advantage of the enlarged forces of production created by capitalism. The utilization of modern industry and technology cannot take place in small and isolated communities. In creating forces of production capable of producing on a scale hitherto unimaginable, capitalism had created a world of interdependencies. To adopt the model of isolated utopian communities was to forswear the advantages of modern technology. Such "small experiments" were "necessarily doomed to failure."[16] And if the pioneer socialists who undertook these experiments sought to reap the advantages of modern technology by entering into the network of interdependencies created by capitalism, they thereby placed themselves under the yoke of competitive markets whose operations were beyond their control.

---

15. For Marx's and Engels's comments on the "socialisms" of Carlyle, Grün, and Sismondi, as well as on other "socialisms" of the mid-nineteenth century, see the section of the *Manifesto* on "Socialist and Communist Literature." The criticism of the socialism of Sismondi sketched in this chapter applies also to the system envisaged by Proudhon, though in the *Manifesto* Marx and Engels raise different objections to the socialism of Proudhon.

16. Marx and Engels, *Manifesto*, p. 40. For "New Jerusalems," see ibid., p. 41.

Related arguments can be made from a Marxist point of view against other socialist visions of the nineteenth century. In 1863 the first workers' political party was formed under the leadership of Ferdinand Lassalle. As we have seen, Lassalle envisaged a society of producers' cooperatives in which the workers owned the enterprises in which they worked. Lassalle sought to align this Workers' Party with the Prussian aristocracy against the rising bourgeoisie and in support of German nationalism under Prussian leadership. In exchange Lassalle tried to get government funding for the creation of producers' cooperatives. From the vantage point of their overview of the course of historical development, Marx and Engels saw Lassalle's plan as a reactionary strategy, aimed at preserving the powers of the Prussian feudal aristocracy and pandering to reactionary nationalism rather than progressive internationalism. They also thought Lassalle was naive in thinking that the Prussian government would support his scheme for producers' cooperatives. And they criticized Lassalle's "iron law of wages," which the Lassalleans took to show the futility of trade unions.[17]

But there is another criticism of the Lassallean vision that runs parallel to Marx's criticism of the petty-bourgeois socialism of Sismondi and the anarchism of Proudhon and that reveals a lot about the Marxist position:

> In [Marx's] view the domination of the economy by producers' associations was simply a repetition of Proudhon's Utopia: units of this kind, even if they belonged to the workers, could only exist in a state of competition like that which now [under capitalism] prevailed. The laws of the market would continue to operate; there would still be crises, bankruptcies, and the concentration of capital.[18]

Forced to respond to the pressures of competitive markets, producer-owned cooperatives would have to behave exactly like capitalist firms.[19] A society organized on this basis would replicate the evils of capitalism.

---

17. Criticisms of Lassalle and the Lassalleans can be found in many of the works of Marx and Engels and in much of their correspondence. The most extended criticism of the Lassallean position comes in Marx's *Critique of the Gotha Programme* (1875) (Moscow: Progress, 1971).

18. Leszek Kolakowski, *Main Currents of Marxism* (Oxford: Clarendon Press, 1978), vol. 1, p. 242.

19. In fact, there would be some differences. On this, see David Schweickart, *Capitalism or Worker Control?* (New York: Praeger, 1980), p. 71f. Whether the differences are sufficient to obviate the Marxist objection raised by Kolakowski is open to question. The system proposed by Schweickart is a complex model of market socialism, designed to avoid some of the difficulties in the simple Lassallean scheme.

This argument nicely illustrates both the deficiencies of the Lassallean and Proudhonian solutions, as viewed from the Marxist perspective, and the Marxist idea that it is the system, and not the greed of individual capitalists, that produces misery for the working class.

Against these various alternative socialisms, Marx and Engels proposed a revolutionary socialism in which the working class seizes political power, expropriates private capital, and democratically controls a planned economy designed to utilize the productive forces developed by capitalism to the benefit of all members of society.

In the *Manifesto*, written at a time when every European country excluded the working class from the right to vote, Marx and Engels depict the proletarian seizure of power in terms of "the violent overthrow of the bourgeoisie."[20] Later, Marx allowed for the possibility that, where the working class had the right to vote, the revolutionary overthrow of the bourgeoisie might be achieved by peaceful means, though even at this later date Marx saw "force" as the more common road to working-class power.[21] In spite of this conviction that revolutionary violence would most likely be necessary for the working-class conquest of power, Marx and Engels steered clear of Blanquist conspiratorial strategies of armed insurrection. Marx and Engels were convinced that working-class conquest of power could only grow out of a mass class-conscious struggle of the working class.

With the development of a revolutionary movement for parliamentary forms of government in Germany, Marx and Engels, together with other of their comrades, returned from exile in London to Germany, settling in Cologne, an industrial center, in April 1848. During the next few months Marx and Engels worked, against some rival leaders of working-class organizations in Cologne, to turn the working-class movement toward an alliance with the revolutionary democratic forces within the bourgeoisie. They also sought to develop forms of cooperative struggle between the working-class organizations of Cologne and peasant organizations in the surrounding countryside. In this organizing work and in their writings for the *Neue Rheinische Zeitung*, edited by Marx, Marx and Engels followed the strategy, set out in the *Manifesto*, of alliance with the progressive bourgeoisie against the remnants of feudalism. They hoped to contribute to a broad-based democratic struggle that would lay the basis for further political action by the

---

20. Marx and Engels, *Manifesto*, p. 21.

21. Karl Marx, "Amsterdam Speech" (September 8, 1872) in Robert Tucker, ed., *The Marx-Engels Reader* (New York: Norton, 1978), p. 523.

working class. Nevertheless, Marx and Engels made clear the distinct interests of the working class and, contrary to the bourgeois democrats in Germany, they outspokenly stood by the workers of Paris following the rising and repression of June.[22]

With the defeat of the democratic movement in Germany, Marx and Engels were forced to return to exile in London. In 1864 Marx looked back on the period following the revolutions of 1848:

> After the failure of the Revolutions of 1848, all party organizations and party journals of the working classes were, on the Continent, crushed by the iron hand of force, the most advanced sons of labour fled in despair to the Transatlantic Republic, and the short-lived dreams of emancipation vanished before an epoch of industrial fever, moral marasme, and political reaction.[23]

In place of the victorious international solidarity of the working class envisaged by the *Manifesto*, there was, Marx said, only the "solidarity of defeat."[24]

After some years of scholarly work amid bitter infighting among the vanquished of 1848, Marx and Engels joined with other working-class leaders in November of 1864 to launch the International Workingmen's Association. With representatives from working-class organizations in Poland, Germany, Italy, France, and England, this First International was formed at a public meeting in London. Marx and Engels had played a central role in preparing for the meeting, which elected George Odger, a British trade unionist, as president of its general council. Marx served as the corresponding secretary for Germany, was one of thirty-four elected to the general council, drafted the rules of the International, and gave the inaugural address.[25]

In this *Inaugural Address* Marx surveyed the fortunes of the European working class since the revolutionary risings of 1848. He pointed to the further concentration of capital and the continued poverty of the working class. He acknowledged that the cooperative movement had been of some value but insisted that so long as the movement aimed at

---

22. See Alan Gilbert, *Marx's Politics* (New Brunswick: Rutgers University Press, 1981), pp. 137-198, for an account of the political strategy of Marx and Engels during the revolutions of 1848.

23. Karl Marx, "Inaugural Address of the Working Men's International Association," in Tucker, *Marx-Engels Reader*, p. 516.

24. Ibid., p. 517.

25. Ibid., pp. 512-519.

the formation of cooperative enterprises within the framework of capitalism, it could not serve as a general means for the emancipation of the working class. Marx argued that emancipation of the working class could be achieved only at the national level. What was required was the conquest of political power by the working class. More important than the cooperative movement, in Marx's eyes, was the passage of the Ten Hours Bill by the English Parliament, for the act "was not only a great practical success; it was the victory of a principle; it was the first time that in broad daylight the political economy of the middle class succumbed to the political economy of the working class."[26] In this and other political struggles Marx thought he saw the seeds of "the political reorganization of the working men's party."[27]

In this positive view of reformist political struggle, some commentators have claimed to find in Marx's own thought a shift from the revolutionary rhetoric of the *Manifesto* in the direction of the reform-minded Social Democratic parties that would represent Marxism after Marx's death. There can be no doubt that the tone of the *Inaugural Address* is less dramatic than the tone of the *Manifesto*, but I believe it is a mistake to see any fundamental shift in Marx's thinking. For one thing, the moderate tone of the *Inaugural Address* can be attributed to Marx's well-known attempt to "frame the thing so that our view should appear in a form acceptable from the present standpoint of the workers' movement."[28] More importantly, the *Inaugural Address*, no less than the *Manifesto*, insists on the key revolutionary principle of political power for the working class. Reforms such as the Ten Hours Bill are heralded not as substitutes for the revolutionary transformation of capitalism but as indicators of the growing political power of the working class.[29] The more important shift in Marx's thinking involves a turn away from the 1848 strategy of alliance with the progressive bourgeoisie against the remnants of feudalism toward a more independent working-class politics. The events of 1848 had shown that the bourgeoisie could not be relied on to act in a consistently progressive way. Although Marx still thought it was correct to side with the bourgeoisie when it acted in a

---

26. Ibid., p. 517.
27. Ibid., p. 518.
28. Marx to Engels, November 4, 1864, in *Marx Engels Selected Correspondence* (Moscow: Progress, 1982), p. 139.
29. Nor should it be forgotten that the *Manifesto* itself includes a surprisingly "moderate" list of initial steps for a proletarian government. It includes, for example, a graduated income tax and public education. See Marx and Engels, *Manifesto*, pp. 30-31.

revolutionary way against feudalism, it was by now clear that workers needed independent organizations to press their own demands.

From the time of its inception the International Workingmen's Association was divided by the different aims of the various groups within it. The strong British contingent was dominated by trade unionists. As we have seen, rudimentary forms of trade union organization had been a part of the British working-class movement since the eighteenth century. Although the legality of strikes remained murky, the trade union movement had continued to gain strength in the intervening years, with the organization of unions for engineers (1851), carpenters (1860), miners (1863), and tailors (1866). By 1868 the movement was strong enough to call for the first Trade Union Congress in Manchester in 1868. Within the British trade union movement there had been an ongoing debate between those who favored "pure and simple" trade unionism and those who favored "political" action. Pure and simple unionism focused on the fight at the work-place for better wages and better working conditions through collective bargaining. The political unionists aimed either at legislative reform by elected political representatives or at revolutionary seizure of political power. With the defeat of the Chartists in 1848 the British trade union movement turned largely to pure-and-simple trade unionism. But by 1864 several trade unionist leaders, some of whom had been active participants in the Chartist movement, were ready to try political action once again. For these trade unionists the turn to political action was seen as a way of promoting the interests of their members. Not really revolutionists, they hoped to use political action to support reforms that would better the lives of their members or the threat of revolutionary political action as leverage to gain full rights of collective bargaining. It was these trade unionists, ready to try the "political" approach, who joined in the formation of the International. With their primary loyalties to the members of their own unions and their pragmatic distrust of intellectuals and theory, these British trade unionists were not strong allies of the revolutionary internationalism of Marx and Engels.[30]

---

30. Strikes were clearly illegal under the Combination Acts of 1799 and 1800. These acts were repealed in 1824, but it was not until the Protection of Property Act of 1875 that trade unions were specifically excluded from laws prohibiting conspiracy in restraint of trade. Whether or not this act of 1875 was in any way an effect of the trade unions' participation in the First International is, of course, another matter. As late as the Taff Vale Judgement of 1901, the British courts held that unions could be sued for losses sustained by a company during a strike.

Theoretical opposition to Marxism came from another current within the First International. In France the anarchism of P. J. Proudhon remained a powerful influence within the working-class movement. These Proudhonists aimed at a mutualist society in which workers owned and controlled the enterprises in which they worked. As anarchists, they were opposed to all forms of political organization that involved the coercive control of human beings. The State, with its apparatus of police, courts, and prisons, they viewed as essentially such an instrument of coercive control. But in rejecting the State they also rejected the Marxist idea of a national, planned economy. In its place the mutualists proposed a federalist society in which all cooperation would rest on the voluntary agreement of the autonomous self-controlled enterprises. Further differences with both the Marxists and the British trade unionists appeared in the tactical stance of the Proudhonists. For as a consequence of their rejection of all coercion and their belief that State power is essentially coercive, they rejected both trade union strikes and political action, whether in its electoral or revolutionary forms.

Yet another theoretical alternative to Marxism within the First International grew out of the anarchism of Mikhail Bakunin. Like Proudhon, Bakunin was an anarchist who rejected any form of the State. His vision of the society of the future was similar to Proudhon's mutualism in its basic outlines. Like Proudhon, he aimed at the formation of a system in which working people controlled the enterprises in which they worked and in which all other social relations were the result of mutual agreements between these autonomous enterprises. But whereas Proudhon relied on moral persuasion as the only morally acceptable means to reach this mutualist society, Bakunin expected the new way of life to appear as the outcome of a violent revolutionary outburst of the international proletariat.

Like Marx and Engels, Bakunin had played an active role in the events of 1848. Having become a revolutionary on philosophical grounds, Bakunin greeted the February rising in Paris with joy and hurried there to join the revolution. Arriving in Paris near the end of February, Bakunin exhorted the workers of Paris to revolutionary victory. As the revolutionary movement spread across Europe from Paris eastward, Bakunin, a Russian Slav, took upon himself the task of arousing the Slavic people. Arriving in Prague, Bakunin took part in a Slav Congress there. And although he had opposed the revolutionary rising by students there on the grounds that their forces were too small, Bakunin joined them on the barricades.[31] With the defeat of the rising in Prague, Bakunin moved to Germany where he participated in risings in Dresden and Chemnitz in spring 1849. Captured by the Prussian authorities, Bakunin was sentenced to death. This sentence was later commuted to life in prison. Having also received a sentence of life in prison from the Austrians for his revolutionary activities there, Bakunin was eventually handed over to the Russian authorities, who banished him to Siberia. Escaping from Siberia on board a U.S. vessel, Bakunin made his way across the United States to England, where he arrived in 1861.

Bakunin's relationship with Marx had not always been one of hostility. He had a great deal of respect for Marx's theoretical abilities. He had met Marx in Paris in 1844 and had accepted Marx's 1847 criticism of Proudhon's reliance on moral persuasion.[32] At one time he also proposed translating *Capital* into Russian. And Marx expressed his own high regard for Bakunin in a letter to Engels around the time of the formation of the International in November of 1864.[33] But within a few years Marx and Bakunin were enemies, and the conflict between them and their followers split the International.

In the years after its formation the International grew with the addition of representatives from working-class organizations in Switzerland, Belgium, Austria, Spain, and Holland. During these years Marx and Engels worked to make the International a centralized organization with a common program of action binding on its member groups. In the early years of the International their chief opposition came from the Proudhonists in France. At the Brussels Congress of the International in September 1868 the Marxist forces won a victory over the Proudhonists with the passage of resolutions calling for the collective ownership of land, forests, mines, roads, and canals and endorsing the use of the strike. But within a year after this victory the Marxists were engaged in a bitter fight with the followers of Bakunin over control of the International.

At a philosophical level, the debate between the Marxists and the anarchists had to do with the nature of the society that would emerge from capitalism. Marx envisaged the proletariat winning political power for itself and using that power to transform the social order and

---

31. "I . . . went with a rifle from one barricade to another, fired a few shots, but was really something of a guest in the whole affair." Bakunin, as quoted in Aileen Kelly, *Mikhail Bakunin* (Oxford: Clarendon Press, 1982), p. 137.

32. Karl Marx, *The Poverty of Philosophy* (New York: International, 1973).

33. Marx to Engels, November 4, 1864 in *Marx Engels Werke*, vol. 31 (Berlin: Dietz Verlag), p. 16.

overcome any counterrevolutionary forces. But this proletarian State was viewed as a transition form only: "When, in the course of development, class distinctions have disappeared, and all production has been concentrated in the hands of a vast association of the whole nation, the public power will lose its political character."[34] In place of the coercive State Marxists looked forward to an eventual communist society in which coercive political power completely disappeared, leaving behind only a cooperative administrative structure by which a rationally planned society could be directed.

The anarchists rejected this strategy. They argued that once established, such a State power, because of its increased control of the economy, would only extend coercive despotism over the masses. They argued that it was unrealistic to think that such a State power would ever be relinquished by those who held it and that the administration of the communist society of the future, even if drawn from the working class, would form interests of its own opposed to the interests of the class as a whole.

To this the Marxists replied that anarchist opposition to a transition form of coercive political control by the working class condemned the working class to remain in its chains. And the Marxists also argued, as they had against the followers of Lassalle, Proudhon, and the cooperative movement in general, that the mutualist society of the anarchists was doomed to failure. If the worker-controlled enterprises of the anarchists stood in market relations with one another, the result would be the same as under capitalism. Only a national approach in which the forces of the market were brought under the rational control of a democratically formed plan could achieve emancipation for the working class as a whole. If the mutualist society envisaged by the anarchists provided for such rational control, then it too must allow for a system of central administration similar to that proposed by the Marxists. If mutualism did not provide for this rational control, it could not hope to achieve the liberation of the working class at which it aimed.

This basic philosophical difference was overlaid with other issues as well. Marx saw Russia as the bastion of reaction and looked to Germany to lead in social revolution. Bakunin saw Germany as the bastion of reaction and pinned his hopes on a revolutionary Russia. In the end the issue that brought the conflict to a head within the International concerned charges by the Marxists that Bakunin and his followers were

---

34. Marx, *Manifesto*, p. 31.

attempting to take over the International and bend it to the service of dubious and ill-considered revolutionary schemes.[35]

At the Hague Congress of the International in September 1872, Bakunin and some of his followers were expelled from the International. But, by this time, the International had ceased to function as an effective working-class organization. In part this was due to the internal conflicts between Marxists and anarchists. In part also it was due to the repression directed at working-class organizations, and in particular at the International, in the months following the rising of the Paris Commune.

In July 1870 war had broken out between Prussia, backed by the other German States, and France under the leadership of the emperor, Napoleon III. By October Napoleon III was a German captive, and the commander of the French forces had surrendered to the Germans. In France a republic was formed, but resistance to the Germans was largely restricted to the armed people of Paris. In January 1871, Paris surrendered, but the people were not disarmed. In March the government of France, now under the leadership of Adolphe Thiers, attempted both to cut off national guard payments and to disarm the people of Paris. Angered by these acts, and by the capitulation of the government to German peace demands, the people of Paris revolted against the Thiers government in Versailles and proclaimed the Paris Commune.

Like the revolutionary rising of 1848, the rising of the Paris Commune in 1871 resulted from a number of complex causes. Those who participated in the Commune were by no means all socialists and were certainly not Marxists. But from the beginning radical working-class demands found expression within the Commune. Among its other acts, for example, the Commune abolished all payments of rent for the period between October 1870 and April 1871, making rents that had been paid apply for future payments. It abolished night work for bakers, provided legal penalties against employers who cheated their workers, and provided for the workers to take over and operate closed workshops and factories.

In its political structure the Commune was radically egalitarian. It provided for the election of all officials by universal manhood suffrage. It restricted officeholders to short terms of office and provided for their

---

35. On the controversy between Marx and Bakunin within the First International, see Kolakowski, *Main Currents*, vol. 1, pp. 246-256, and Kelly, *Mikhail Bakunin*, pp. 227-237.

recall. And it limited the salaries paid to officials to the level of salaries paid to workmen.

The Commune also expressed an international spirit. It permitted the election of foreigners residing in Paris to its governing bodies. Among its first acts was the abolishment of conscription. And in May 1871, the Commune approved the pulling down of the Vendôme column, a monument erected to commemorate French military victories.

The Thiers government moved to crush the rebellion in Paris. There followed a protracted battle in which much of working-class Paris was destroyed. Brutalities were committed by both sides. In retaliation for the execution of captured Communards, the Commune proclaimed its intent to take hostages. Some sixty-four hostages were killed, including the archbishop of Paris and the commander of the national guard. But in the end the Commune was crushed. Some 20,000 Communards were executed, and many more died in prison colonies outside France. Altogether Paris lost some 50,000 workers and political activists.[36]

In the months that followed, repression was directed at all those who had supported the Commune. Although Marx had himself opposed the rising as futile, once the action was taken, members of the International-- including Marx's son-in-law, Paul Lafargue--played an active if minor role in the life of the Commune, and Marx himself wrote a defense of the Commune as a heroic act of the revolutionary working class.[37] In any case, with the defeat of the Commune the International Workingmen's Association became the target for repressive measures, both in France and in other countries. In 1876 it was officially dissolved.

Marx died on March 14, 1883. At the time of his death the cause for which he had devoted his life appeared to be largely defeated. But by the turn of the century the ideas of Marx and Engels had garnered the support of a revived socialist movement. In the Second International the socialist theories of Marx and Engels found widespread support in a powerful international alliance of political parties committed to the cause of the working class. In the next chapter we will examine this Second International. In retrospect, the period of the Second International appears to be the golden age of European socialism.[38]

---

36. Albert S. Lindemann, *A History of European Socialism* (New Haven: Yale University Press, 1983), p. 129.

37. Karl Marx, *The Civil War in France* (1871) (Moscow: Progress, 1974).

38. Leszek Kolakowski, *Main Currents*, vol. 2, p. 1, calls this period "the golden age of Marxism." I believe it was also the golden age of European socialism.

4

The Socialism
of the Second International

In May 1863, under the leadership of Ferdinand Lassalle, the first working-class political party in Germany was formed, the General Association of German Workers. As we have already seen, this party sought State support for the formation of producers' cooperatives that would be owned and controlled by the workers. It sought the right to vote for its members, but it rejected the trade union movement and strikes by workers as futile acts within the structure of capitalism, where, according to Lassalle, an "iron law" of wages prevailed, keeping wage rates at subsistence levels. The party was strongly nationalistic, holding that Germany was destined to provide the spiritual leadership for the rest of the world. Politically, the party was aligned with the conservative aristocracy against the liberal bourgeoisie. It remained independent of the International Workingmen's Association--the First International-- which had been formed a year later.

Marx and Engels were highly critical of this political party. Against the Lassalleans, they supported the trade union movement and strikes by trade unions aimed at improving the lot of the working class. They rejected the Lassallean view that such actions were futile within the confines of capitalism and supported trade union struggles aimed at better wages for workers.[1] They criticized Lassalle's flirtation with the Prussian aristocracy and advocated alliance with the progressive bourgeoisie against this aristocracy. They also championed an internationalist viewpoint against Lassalle's pandering to German nationalism. And finally, as we have already seen, they rejected the

---

1. For the theoretical reasoning behind the Marxist position here, see Karl Marx, *Value Price and Profit* (1865) (New York: International, 1974).

Lassallean plan for a system of producers' cooperatives as incapable of realizing the emancipation of the working class as a whole.

As a result of these differences, supporters of the Marxist approach in Germany organized a second German workers' party--the German Social Democratic Workers Party--in August 1869. This party was under the leadership of Wilhelm Liebknecht and August Bebel. Liebknecht, who was well educated and spoke fluent French and English, at the age of twenty-three had participated in an armed rising in Baden during fall 1848. Forced into exile, he met Marx and Engels in England. Eventually he was allowed to return to Germany, where he settled in Leipzig and devoted himself to the cause of the working class. In Leipzig he met August Bebel. Bebel was a carpenter of working-class origins who became active in working-class politics in the early 1860s. Convinced by Liebknecht of the correctness of Marxism, he joined Liebknecht in bringing the Marxist analysis to the German working class. Both Liebknecht and Bebel were elected to the North German Diet in 1867. Both had opposed the war with Austria in 1866 and both opposed the war against France in 1870, refusing to vote for funding for the war effort and condemning the German annexation of Alsace-Lorraine. Eventually Bebel was convicted of treason for his antiwar efforts and sentenced to four years in prison.[2]

This opposition to the war with France brought international recognition and respect for Liebknecht and Bebel from socialists outside Germany. And following the extension of the franchise to cover the national parliament of the newly united Germany, Liebknecht and Bebel were regularly reelected to this national parliament by their working-class supporters in Germany. The two maintained close ties with Marx and Engels in England and gradually succeeded in establishing the Social Democratic Workers party as a strong Marxist political party in Germany. Following the death of the charismatic Lassalle in a duel in 1863, his followers entered into a protracted contest with the Marxists for the support of the German working class. The Marxists won out and at Gotha, in 1875, the remnants of Lassalle's party united with the Marxists under the leadership of Liebknecht and Bebel.[3]

The united Social Democrats grew in strength. In an effort to stop the socialists, the German government used the pretext of an attempt on the

2.   James Joll, *The Second International* (New York: Harper Colophon, 1966), pp. 9-10.

3.   Marx was himself incensed at the concessions made to the Lassalleans in the program adopted at Gotha and wrote a scathing, unpublished attack upon it. Marx, *Critique of the Gotha Programme* (1875) (Moscow: Progress, 1971).

emperor's life, an attempt in which the Social Democrats were in no way involved, as a pretext for antisocialist laws. Party meetings, organizations, and publications were outlawed, and leaders of the party were forced into exile. In spite of this repression the party survived and indeed grew. When the antisocialist laws were lifted in 1890, the Social Democrats received nearly 1.5 million votes and won thirty-five seats in the Reichstag.

The following year, at a party congress in Erfurt, the Social Democrats dropped the Lassallean ideas from their program and emerged with a program that received the endorsement of Engels.[4] This Erfurt Program contained a preamble that spelled out a Marxist analysis of capitalism, stressing the inevitable concentration of wealth, the inevitability of crises, increasing unemployment, and the relative poverty of workers and framing all of these observations in terms of the sharpening contradictions between the forces and relations of production. The program formulated a primary aim of the winning of power by the working class and the socializing of the economy, but it also supported the fight for reforms so long as capitalism remained. It took a clear internationalist and antimilitarist stance. And it included a list of demands: universal suffrage, direct secret ballot, proportional representation, replacement of the army by an armed citizenry, freedom of speech and assembly, equal rights for women, compulsory and free public education, abolition of the state church and establishment of religious freedom, public legal and medical care, progressive taxation, the eight-hour day, abolition of child labor under the age of fourteen, and regulation of working conditions.

On the basis of this program, the Social Democrats advanced in strength. In 1890 they received 1.4 million votes. Growing steadily, these vote totals reached 3.0 million in 1903 and 4.25 million in 1912. By 1912 the Social Democrats polled one-third of the total vote and had became the largest party bloc in the Reichstag.

In keeping with the Marxist position, the Social Democrats supported the trade union movement. The party provided funds and organizers to assist in the formation of unions and gave union leaders positions of power within the party. In this way the party sought to overcome the split between "pure and simple" and "political" alternatives within the working-class movement. Although not without its tensions and difficulties, this dual strategy of trade union organization and electoral politics worked to cement the ties between the party and the working

---

4. Marx had died in 1883.

class and gave the party a distinctive identity that distinguished its nature from all other political parties.

In addition to the trade unions, the party organized and supported a wide variety of publications, training schools, athletic clubs, social clubs, debating societies, theatrical troupes, women's organizations, and youth groups. These organizations served the needs of workers and their families, strengthened the influence of the party within the working class, and, in effect, created a working-class culture with its own identity and sense of purpose.

This strong and richly developed German Social Democratic Party became the model for the formation of Social Democratic parties in Austria, France, Belgium, Holland, Italy, Poland, Russia, and other countries, including England and the United States. Even before the German party officially approved the Erfurt Program in 1891, in 1889 representatives from these parties met at an international congress in Paris where they formed the Second International. Unlike the First International, the Second International consisted of affiliated political parties; but like the First International, the general aim of the Second International was to facilitate cooperation between the workers' movements in different countries, to share information, and to discuss common problems and strategies for solving them.

Although not without its disagreements and its dissenting voices, the socialists of the Second International were far more cohesive in outlook than were the socialists of the First International. There were several reasons for this. First, by this time the Marxist perspective had achieved a kind of theoretical hegemony over most socialist groups. Second, this hegemony was in part the result of the historical developments within the working-class movement that seemed largely to confirm the Marxist analysis. For example, the experiments with labor exchanges and utopian communities had been made and abandoned. On the other hand, it was becoming clear that the trade union movement was going to last. Any serious working-class party would have to find a place in its outlook for trade unions--something that, for example, neither the anarchism of Proudhon nor the cooperationism of Lassalle could do. Further, with the extension of the franchise to members of the working class in many of the European countries, anarchist opposition to electoral politics appeared increasingly untenable. Another factor had to do with the very success of the German model. In the last decade of the nineteenth century it seemed that in that model the socialist movement had found the vehicle that would take it to power. All of these factors helped to provide a greater theoretical unity to the socialists of the Second International. It also helped that an alternative international socialist meeting was called for Paris at the same time. This alternative meeting, which did not give rise to any long-lasting organization, drained off elements of the international movement who were not in sympathy with the Marxist approach.[5]

The Social Democrats of the Second International accepted the Marxist analysis according to which the natural tendencies of capitalism are toward concentration and centralization of capital, increasing unemployment, polarization of classes, increasing and deepening crises, and relative poverty for the masses. They believed that the historical development of capitalism revealed these tendencies and so gradually created in the proletariat a consciousness of the necessity of a proletarian revolution aimed at the overthrow of capitalism and its replacement by a socialist economic system. They believed that this socialism involved public ownership of the means of production and the employment of these resources according to a rational plan for the good of all members of society. They believed that this socialism also involved democratic control of the economy. They were *social* democrats who aimed at the extension of the principle of democratic control beyond the elections of political officials to the additional "social questions" of economic life that had come to the fore in the nineteenth century. They were social *democrats* who believed that socialist control of the means of production could be achieved only on the basis of popular elections; freedom of speech, press, and assembly; and the absence of discrimination on the basis of race, sex, or religion. They believed that socialism meant the elimination of militarism and standing armies. They believed that the fight for socialism must involve a struggle for immediate reforms within the framework of capitalism, but they also believed it must involve a struggle for political power and the consequent revolutionary transformation of the social order. They believed that capitalism would be swept away when the proletariat became conscious of the impossibility of fully solving its problems within the framework of capitalism. And finally, from all of this, and from their understanding of the ongoing nature of the existing class struggle and the possibilities open to them, they drew the conclusion that the way ahead lay in the dual strategy of trade unionism and electoral politics.

Not all socialists in the last decade of the nineteenth century agreed with this strategy. Anarchism remained a force in the working-class movement, especially in Spain and Italy. At a theoretical level the

---

5.   On this alternative International, see Joll, chap. 2.

Russian anarchist Peter Kropotkin developed the philosophical foundations of anarchism to their highest level of expression.

In France an alternative socialist perspective emerged in the form of syndicalism. (A *syndicat ouvrier* is simply a trade union.) Syndicalism can be understood as socialism built on the trade unions. The idea was for each union to take over and manage its sector of the economy. Matters involving outside sectors would be worked out in cooperation with representatives from the other unions. In a sense, syndicalism represented a resurgence of the Proudhonist idea of federative mutualism, only now the units of mutual cooperation were understood to be unions instead of individual enterprises. In the years between 1900 and World War I, revolutionary syndicalist ideas spread throughout much of the industrialized world. The Industrial Workers of the World (IWW), born in the United States in 1905, was heavily influenced by these syndicalist ideas.

Another alternative to the Marxist orthodoxy of the Second International was provided by the Fabian socialists in England. Organized in 1883, the Fabian Society was conceived as a society for research and propaganda rather than as a political party. (The English Social Democratic Federation, founded in 1881, was the Social Democratic Party in England.) With an illustrious membership that included George Bernard Shaw, H. G. Wells, and Sidney and Beatrice Webb, the Fabians produced a great deal of valuable research and propaganda. The Fabians acknowledged their intellectual debt to Marx and shared much of the Marxist analysis of capitalism as well as the Marxist support for trade unions, electoral politics, and an eventual planned economy. But there were important differences with the Marxists. The Fabians were much more interested than the Marxists in the moral case for socialism. They argued that capitalism was fundamentally unjust: Those who worked received little, and those who received the most did not work. They also thought that democracy was morally desirable and that since only socialism extended democracy to economic matters, only socialism was morally acceptable. Because of this concern for questions of morality, and because also of their doubt of the economic inevitability of socialism, the Fabians stressed the role of moral persuasion in the coming of socialism. They rejected any revolutionary insurrectionism as both unnecessary and as morally unacceptable. They were also more sympathetic than the Marxists to the prospects for local forms of cooperative control.

These Fabian ideas influenced the thinking of the German Social Democrat, Eduard Bernstein. Bernstein was a party journalist who was in exile in England during the period of the antisocialist laws. While there, he became close to Engels, so close that it was to him that Engels bequeathed the papers of Marx and Engels upon Engels's death. But while in England Bernstein also came under the influence of the Fabians. Their arguments, and his own view of the world around him, convinced him that Marxism was seriously flawed. Soon after Engels's death in 1895, Bernstein published a series of articles in *Die Neue Zeit*, the leading theoretical journal of the Second International.[6] In these articles Bernstein argued that Marx was clearly wrong on a number of points. Contrary to Marx, the working class had improved its standard of living. The middle class had not disappeared. Small businesses had not disappeared. And the development of banking and credit institutions had brought the tendency toward crises under control. For all these reasons Marx was fundamentally wrong in thinking that socialism was the inevitable outcome of capitalism. Bernstein blamed Marx's mistakes on what Bernstein saw as Marx's dogmatic reliance on Hegelian dialectics, a metaphysical certainty of historical progress. In place of this metaphysical dogma, Bernstein recommended that Social Democrats rely on modern social science.

However, although he rejected Marx's claim to have provided scientific proof for the inevitability of socialism, Bernstein did not abandon the cause of socialism. Instead, he argued that socialism, though not a scientific necessity, was a moral necessity. Like the Fabians, Bernstein proposed to replace Marx's "scientific socialism" with an "ethical socialism." In this matter, as well as in his criticisms of Marxist science, Bernstein followed not only the Fabian socialists but also criticisms of the social democrats coming from some sympathetic academic philosophers.[7] The basic idea of this "ethical socialism" was that the coming of socialism was not inevitable and depended on moral persuasion. But the ethical socialists also felt uncomfortable with the revolutionary rhetoric of the Marxists. Bernstein rejected the insurrectionist model for the coming of socialism as both unrealistic and morally unacceptable. In place of a rapid, violent, revolutionary change from capitalism to socialism, he argued for a gradual, peaceful, evolutionary process of change. In fact, Bernstein argued, this was the

---

6.   An English language version of these articles was published in 1899 under the title of *Evolutionary Socialism*. See Eduard Bernstein, *Evolutionary Socialism* (New York: Schocken, 1961).

7.   The principal critics were Friedrich Albert Lange, Hermann Cohen, and Karl Vorländer. For more on this subject, see Richard Hudelson, *Marxism and Philosophy in the Twentieth Century* (New York: Praeger, 1990), chap. 1.

path on which the party had embarked. What was needed was a change to bring the party's theory more in line with its actual practice.

Bernstein's "revisionism" raised a storm of controversy within the German party and within the Second International.[8] Karl Kautsky, the editor of *Die Neue Zeit* and the leading theoretician of the Second International, led the defense of Marxist orthodoxy.[9] Kautsky was supported within the German party by Liebknecht and Bebel. Another faction within the German party, led by Rosa Luxemburg, challenged Bernstein's analysis from a different point of view. Although she agreed with Kautsky in rejecting Bernstein's plea for a change in theory, she agreed with Bernstein that the party's practice had deviated from its theory. She concluded that what was needed was not less revolutionary theory but more revolutionary practice.[10]

These "revisionism debates" spilled over into the international arena where, among others, V. I. Lenin firmly supported the revolutionary side in the debates. In the end, the orthodox center won out. At international congress after international congress, Social Democrats reaffirmed their Marxist orthodoxy and their confidence in the direction of party policies. In spite of their theoretical and practical squabbles, Social Democrats in 1912 could look on the world with pride in what they had achieved and with confidence in their eventual victory.

Even in the United States the socialism of the Second International had gained a foothold. Socialism and the labor movement in the United States faced a hostile ideological environment. U.S. law and the courts backed up a principled commitment to laissez faire capitalism, founded on the social Darwinist conviction that welfare state intervention in the economy weakened the fabric of the nation, long after most of the European states had abandoned this position. The refusal of the law to clearly recognize the rights of working people to bargain collectively with their employers led to a high level of violence in American industrial disputes. In the late 1870s nineteen men were hanged for their leadership of the Molly Maguires in the coal fields of Pennsylvania.[11]

---

8. For some of the principal documents from this debate, see H. Tudor and J. M. Tudor, eds., *Marxism and Social Democracy: The Revisionism Debate 1896-1898* (Cambridge: Cambridge University Press, 1988).

9. On Kautsky, see Massimo Salvadori, *Karl Kautsky and the Socialist Revolution 1880-1938* (London: NLB, 1979).

10. Rosa Luxemburg, "Reform or Revolution" (1900), in Mary-Alice Waters, ed., *Rosa Luxemburg Speaks* (New York: Pathfinder, 1970).

11. Richard Boyer and Herbert Morais, *Labor's Untold Story* (New York: United Electrical, Radio and Machine Workers of America, 1979), pp. 56-58.

Scores of workers were killed and hundreds wounded in the railroad strike of 1877.[12] In 1886, in many cities of the United States, violent conflicts broke out between the Knights of Labor and local militias. At Haymarket Square in Chicago in that same year, when police attempted to break up a demonstration in support of the eight-hour day, a bomb was thrown, killing seven policemen and leading to the execution of four innocent anarchist leaders. At the Carnegie steel mills in Homestead, Pennsylvania, Pinkerton detectives hired by the steel company opened fire on striking steel workers who were trying to prevent strike-breakers from entering the mills. In the ensuing battle seven strikers and three detectives were killed. Five days later, on July 11, 1892, fighting broke out in Coeur d'Alene, Idaho, between striking miners and strikebreakers, leading to the dispatch of regular army troops to the area and the arrest of 1,200 strikers.[13] Western mining regions were particularly violence ridden. In 1903-1904, armed conflict between miners, on the one side, and private detectives and federal army troops, on the other side, left 42 dead and 112 wounded.[14]

The Pullman strike of 1894 was yet another episode in this saga of industrial violence. The railroad industry had been at the center of the great upheaval in 1877. Railroad workers faced long hours on dangerous jobs. Repeatedly forced to take wage cuts, railroad workers were driven to organize to defend themselves. But because railroad workers were divided into different craft unions--engineers, conductors, brakemen, switchmen, and firemen, each in separate unions--railroad strikes had often failed. Based on his experience with the locomotive firemen's union, Eugene V. Debs became convinced of the necessity for joint action by all railroad workers. Unable to convince the leaders of the railroad unions, in 1893 Debs led the formation of the American Railway Union (ARU), which aimed at organizing the railroads along an "industrial" basis that would include all workers in the industry in one union.

In Spring 1894, the ARU led a successful strike against the Great Northern Railroad. On the basis of this success, enthusiasm for the union swelled among railroad workers. When George Pullman forced wage cuts and layoffs on the already hard-pressed employees of the

---

12. Ibid., p. 59.

13. Ibid., p. 112. For an account of the effect of the Homestead strike on the young anarchists Emma Goldman and Alexander Berkman, see Emma Goldman, *Living My Life*, vol. 1 (New York: Dover, 1970), pp. 83-107. The twenty-one-year-old Berkman was sentenced to 22 years in prison for his attempt to assassinate Henry Clay Frick, Carnegie's lieutenant at Homestead.

14. Boyer and Morais, *Labor's Untold Story*, p. 142.

Pullman Sleeping Car Company, they went out on strike and appealed to the ARU for support. The ARU did its best to support the strike, in spite of its limited resources. Refusing to move trains with Pullman cars attached, the ARU tied up rail traffic in much of the Midwest. Attempts to move the trains with scab crews led to violent confrontations between strikers and detectives hired by the railroad companies. At the request of railroad company officials, President Grover Cleveland ordered the use of federal troops to move the trains and a federal judge granted an injunction ordering the ARU to abandon the strike. Debs and other ARU officials defied the injunction. The strike was violently suppressed. In a series of confrontations, thirty men and women were killed and more injured. Debs and other union officials were sent to jail.

Debs claimed to have been converted to socialism while in jail by reading works of Karl Kautsky, the Marxist theoretician of the Second International, and three volumes of Marx's own *Capital* given to Debs by the Milwaukee socialist Victor Berger.[15] Out of jail, Debs led in the formation of the Social Democratic Party in 1898. In 1901 this party joined with socialists unhappy with the sectarian direction of the Socialist Labor Party, a party rooted historically among German immigrants to the United States, to form the Socialist Party of America.

The Socialist Party was committed to political action. It aimed at the winning of power by the working class and the establishment of a planned socialist economy. In this broad aim the party was aligned with the Marxist current of European socialism prevailing throughout the period of the Second International, though the U.S. party was far from purely Marxist in its make-up, including Christian socialist, populist, and other currents as well. Like its European sister parties, the U.S. party also pressed for immediate reforms, such as welfare aid to the elderly, infirm, and unemployed; child labor laws; and municipal ownership of utilities.

One respect in which the U.S. party differed from the European model was in its relationship to the trade union movement. In the European countries the trade unions were, for the most part, involved in the Social Democratic movement. Social Democrats served as leaders of trade unions, and leaders of trade unions served on the inner councils of the party organizations. Members of the trade unions were apt to be members of the Social Democratic parties and apt to vote for Social Democrats in elections. In contrast, although socialists had a significant

---

15. Nick Salvatore, *Eugene V. Debs* (Urbana: University of Illinois Press, 1982), p. 150. Salvatore questions whether this conversion was as clean as Debs and others have claimed.

presence in U.S. trade unions, in the United States the trade union movement remained independent of and opposed to the socialists, following the "pure and simple" trade unionism of Samuel Gompers, the long-time president of the American Federation of Labor (AFL).[16]

Because of the conservative direction of the U.S. labor movement, radicals of various stripes--socialists and anarchists among them--joined together to organize the Industrial Workers of the World in Chicago in 1905. The preamble of the Industrial Workers of the World proclaimed its revolutionary intent:

> The working class and the employing class have nothing in common. There can be no peace so long as hunger and want are found among millions of working people and the few, who make up the employing class, have all the good things of life. Between these two classes a struggle must go on until the workers of the world organize as a class, take possession of the earth and the machinery of production, and abolish the wage system. . . . It is the historic mission of the working class to do away with capitalism.[17]

Eschewing electoral politics in favor of syndicalism, the IWW called on workers to take direct action. A group of talented and charismatic organizers crisscrossed the country fighting for textile workers, lumberjacks, woodworkers, dockworkers, seamen, iron miners, and agricultural workers. They came to the aid of the great mass of working men and women who stood outside the protection of the existing unions and who were largely ignored by the existing unions. The IWW found organizers who could speak Italian, or Serbian or Croatian, or Yiddish, Polish, Finnish, or Russian. These IWW organizers reached out to the immigrant workers who manned (and womaned) U.S. industry. The IWWs, the Wobblies, filled the jails fighting for freedom of speech in many American cities. Their songs were heard on many picket lines. Their spirit is captured by IWW songwriter Joe Hill who supposedly said, soon before his death by a firing squad in Utah, "Don't mourn,

---

16. On Gompers, see Bernard Mandel, *Samuel Gompers* (Yellow Springs: Antioch Press), 1963.

17. Fred Thompson, *The I.W.W.: Its First Fifty Years* (Chicago: Industrial Workers of the World, 1955), p. 4.

organize!" From their ranks, later, would come many of the members of the American Communist Party.[18]

Meanwhile, in the decade before the first world war the Socialist Party of America carried on a campaign for socialism rooted in electoral politics. In Eugene V. Debs it found a standard-bearer who could bring the message of socialism to American audiences. With the support of intellectuals like Jack London, Upton Sinclair, Carl Sandberg, Helen Keller, Margaret Sanger, and John Reed, it gained access to virtually all corners of American cultural life. During the period from 1900 to 1912, support for the party grew steadily. In the first presidential campaign of 1900, Debs garnered 95,000 votes. By 1912, with over 300 Socialist Party newspapers across the nation, Debs' campaign won 900,000 votes and thousands of Socialists were elected to public office.[19]

Although the American Socialist Party was less of a political force than its European sisters, even U.S. socialists could, in 1912, look to the future with a not unreasonable confidence in their eventual victory. Two years later, in August 1914, war broke out in Europe. The war created an immediate crisis for European Social Democrats, and it set loose forces that would deeply divide the international socialist movement. It is to the war and the division it produced that we now turn.

---

18. On the IWW, in addition to Thompson, see Melvyn Dubofsky, *We Shall Be All* (Chicago: Quadrangle, 1969); Len DeCaux, *The Living Spirit of the Wobblies* (New York: International, 1978); Patrick Renshaw, *The Wobblies* (Garden City: Anchor, 1968).

19. On the Socialist Party of America in this period, see Salvatore, *Eugene V. Debs*, chaps. 8, 9; Paul Buhle, *Marxism in the United States* (London: Verso, 1991), chap. 3; Mari Jo Buhle, *Women and American Socialism* (Urbana: University of Illinois Press, 1983); Elliot Shore, *Talking Socialism* (Lawrence: University Press of Kansas, 1988), on *Appeal to Reason*, the most important of the socialist newspapers; Donald T. Critchlow, ed., *Socialism in the Heartland: The Midwestern Experience 1900-1925* (Notre Dame: University of Notre Dame Press, 1986); and Richard Judd, *Socialist Cities* (Albany: State University of New York Press, 1989).

5

War and Revolution

In the years just prior to World War I socialists could look to the past with pride in what they had achieved and to the future with confidence in their eventual victory. In Germany the Social Democratic trade unions had grown strong, and each election strengthened the Social Democratic Party. And although other countries lagged behind developments in Germany, even in such "primitive" countries as the United States, the socialists had made substantial gains.

The war itself came as no surprise to the Social Democrats. Marxist theory predicted military conflict as the likely outcome of economic competition in advanced capitalism. Indeed, the Second International had so clearly recognized the likelihood of war that, for a decade before the war, it had devoted considerable thought to the questions of how Social Democrats might work to prevent war and how Social Democrats should respond in the event of outbreak of war. At the Congress of the International in Stuttgart in 1907 the Socialists committed the working class and its parliamentary representatives in each country "to do everything to prevent the outbreak of war by whatever means seem to them most effective." Further, the congress went on to resolve that "should war break out in spite of all this, it is their duty to intercede for its speedy end, and to strive with all their power to make use of the violent economic and political crisis brought about by the war to rouse the people, and thereby to hasten the abolition of capitalist class rule."[1] And at an emergency congress of the International, convened in Basel in November 1913, delegates reaffirmed their commitments to the antiwar principles of Stuttgart and other congresses of the International.

But war came. And in each country the war was greeted with an outpouring of patriotic fervor. Social Democrats faced a difficult

---

1.   James Joll, *The Second International* (New York: Harper Colophon, 1966), p. 198.

situation. If they remained true to their principles, they risked alienating their supporters and being repressed as traitors. In country after country Social Democratic parties abandoned their principles and rallied to their respective flags.

One of the few Social Democratic groups to oppose the war was the Bolshevik faction of the Russian Social Democratic Labor Party. As the war developed, tsarist Russia suffered enormous casualties and economic disintegration. In February 1917 an outraged public and rebellious army combined to overthrow the tsar. In November 1917, in "ten days that shook the world," the Bolshevik revolution established the first socialist state.[2] This breach in the world capitalist system would have far-reaching consequences for the worldwide socialist movement.

The Bolshevik revolution cannot be understood in separation from the Russian revolutionary tradition. In December 1825 a group of young army officers, infected with the revolutionary ideas derived from the French revolution, attempted to overthrow the tsar. From that time on, both a sense of the backwardness of Russian political institutions and a revolutionary commitment to change them spread among the Russian intelligentsia. Many of Russia's educated young men and women responded to Alexander Herzen's call for Russian revolutionaries to "go to the people." In this case, the people were overwhelmingly peasants, freed from serfdom only by the reforms of Tsar Nicholas II in 1861. In the 1860s and early 1870s an underground populist movement sent many young revolutionaries into the countryside, where they called upon the peasants to revolt against the tsar and the landed gentry and build a rural-based cooperative society.

In the mid 1870s tsarist officials made a concerted effort to repress this revolutionary populism. Hundreds of Russia's finest young people were sent into exile in Siberia. In response to this repression the Russian populists split into two groups: one determined to fight back by terrorist attacks on tsarist officials; the other resolved to resist by means of agitation. Among those who favored the path of agitation was Georgy Plekhanov, soon to become the "father of Russian Marxism." Among those who favored terrorism was Alexander Ulyanov, older brother of Vladimir Ulyanov, later known to the world as Lenin.

In 1880 Plekhanov was forced into exile where he came into contact with Marxist groups and, in 1883, along with other exiled Russian revolutionaries, formed the Emancipation of Labor Group, a Marxist

---

2.   John Reed, *Ten Days That Shook the World* (1919) (New York: Vintage, 1960), provides a first-hand account of the Bolshevik revolution by a sympathetic U.S. journalist.

social democratic organization. In 1887 Lenin's older brother was hanged for his part in a plot to assassinate Tsar Alexander III.

Aroused by the execution of his brother, Lenin became involved in the revolutionary movement in his teens. Around 1890, at the age of twenty, Lenin adopted Marxism on the basis of his reading of Marx and Plekhanov. By the end of the decade he was one of the leaders of Russian Marxism and a veteran of prison and Siberian exile. As a Marxist, he rejected populist hope for an agrarian cooperative society as a romantic illusion founded on ignorance of the laws of historical development. In his view, the future lay in a modern industrial society governed by the working class. But like many of his contemporary Marxists, Lenin thought that intellectuals played a key role in bringing about socialist proletarian democracy. Lenin thought that, left to themselves, workers would rise to a consciousness of the necessity of trade unions and collective action to defend their economic interests, but only intellectuals--with education, time for study, and an understanding of the general laws of historical development--could see the necessity for revolutionary overthrow of the capitalist system as a whole. Lenin saw it as the task of the revolutionary intelligentsia to bring this revolutionary consciousness to the working class.

Even more important for the future course of socialism was Lenin's conception of the role of the Social Democratic party as developed in *What Is To Be Done?* (1902). In the German model, more or less copied by Social Democratic parties around the world, the party served as a mass party engaged in electoral politics and was surrounded by a network of trade unions, cultural organizations, and party newspapers. In tsarist Russia, where there were no representative institutions and no elections, where unions and party clubs were illegal and infiltrated by police spies, and where there was no freedom of speech or freedom of the press, the German model was dangerously inapplicable. In its place Lenin proposed a small party of committed revolutionaries, operating largely in small secret groups and connected by disciplined adherence to a central party leadership. Lenin argued that only such a party could hope to survive and prevail against the backward political institutions of tsarist Russia. At the Second Congress of the Russian Social Democratic Labor Party, in 1903, the Russian Marxists split into two camps: the Bolsheviks, who agreed with Lenin; and the Mensheviks, who did not.[3]

---

3. Leszek Kolakowski, *Main Currents of Marxism* (Oxford: Clarendon Press, 1978), vol. 2, chaps. 15-16, provides an account of the origins of Marxism and Leninism in Russia. Alfred Meyer, *Leninism* (New York: Praeger, 1967), provides an excellent account of Lenin's

One of the issues of central importance for Russian Marxists concerned the possibilities for revolutionary socialism in backward Russia. The Russian populists had hoped for a uniquely Russian path to socialism, built upon the communal heritage of precapitalist peasant villages. In arguing against the populists, Lenin and other Marxists had depicted this hope as contrary to a law of historical development, discovered by Marx, according to which every society passes through a series of distinct forms of socioeconomic organization: primitive communism, ancient slavery, feudalism, capitalism, and socialism. According to this standpoint, turn-of-the-century Russia was just emerging from feudalism into capitalism and, consequently, was not ready for socialism.

Marx himself rejected this rigid sequence of stages as a mistaken interpretation of his views, explicitly denying any claim to have established a universal law of historical development, claiming for Russia "the finest chance ever offered by history to a people" to escape "all the fatal vicissitudes of the capitalist regime," and specifically suggesting that the peasant communities might serve as "the fulcrum of Russia's social revival."[4] But Marx's letters on this point were not widely known inside or outside Russia, and the sequential schema was taken to be orthodox Marxism by both friends and foes alike.

However, even within this supposed orthodoxy, different interpretations were possible. Some Russian Marxists, such as Peter Struve, looked for a long period of capitalism with socialism arriving in Russia only as the result of a distant evolutionary process. Such a viewpoint confined Social Democrats in Russia to support for the bourgeois revolution against feudalism. But some Marxists, like Rosa Luxemburg, and the Russians Alexander Parvus and Leon Trotsky, argued that in Russia revolutionary overthrow of the tsarist regime might well set in motion a "permanent revolution" leading rapidly from the feudal present to the socialist future. There were several reasons for thinking this. First, the Russian proletariat had the advantage of

---

ideas. A brief overview of the origins of Leninism is provided by Adam Westoby, *The Evolution of Communism* (New York: Free Press, 1989), pp. 17-32. An accessible and entertaining introduction to Lenin's thought and its historical context is provided by Richard Appignanesi and Oscar Zarate in *Lenin for Beginners* (New York: Pantheon, 1978).

4.   Marx to the Editorial Board of *Otechestvenniye Zapiski*, November 1877 (not mailed by Marx but a copy mailed by Engels to Vera Zasulich, March 6, 1884). See Karl Marx and Frederick Engels, *Marx Engels Selected Correspondence* (Moscow: Progress, 1982), for the dates in question. On the peasant commune as the "fulcrum," see Marx's letter to Vera Zasulich, March 8, 1881, in the same volume.

knowing, by the examples of the various Western European countries, the unhappy fate that unfettered capitalism offered them. Second, having come later to Russia than to other countries, capitalism in Russia assumed an "advanced" form, with huge factories where masses of workers in key cities formed a potential revolutionary base. Third, in order to overthrow feudalism, the bourgeoisie required the support of the proletariat. But being much larger than the bourgeoisie, the proletariat, conscious of its world historical position, would not relinquish the historical stage to the bourgeoisie but would push forward toward a socialist future.

Lenin advanced a somewhat different, but also revolutionary, viewpoint. In spite of his opposition to the agrarian communalism of the Russian populists, Lenin recognized the revolutionary potential of the vast Russian peasantry. Accordingly, Lenin argued for an alliance between workers and peasants, both as a strategy for revolutionary upheaval and as the basis for a postrevolutionary society in which political power remained in the hands of the producers rather than their capitalist exploiters. In this respect Lenin, too, envisaged a revolutionary process that went far beyond the bourgeois overthrow of feudalism. But he differed from Parvus and Trotsky in giving the peasantry a share of political power in the postrevolutionary society. This view of Lenin's was criticized by Trotsky and others on the grounds that the peasantry, being a class of small property owners, would oppose the proletarian effort to push the revolutionary process in the direction of socialism.[5]

These theoretical disputes became pressing practical issues in the revolutionary struggles of 1917. Angered by the war, in which Russian casualties were enormous, and exhausted by the breakdown of the economic system, masses of Russians took to the streets in a series of strikes and demonstrations. This time, in contrast to the similar upheavals of 1905, the tsar's armed forces refused to fire on the people. In February the tsar resigned. Eventually a government was formed headed by Aleksandr Kerensky, who, though a "socialist," accepted the prevailing view that Russia was not ripe for socialism, needing first to pass through a capitalist stage of development. The Kerensky

---

5. Fuller discussion of these debates can be found in Westoby, *Evolution of Communism*, pp. 163-171 and in Kolakowski, *Main Currents*, vol. 2, pp. 405-412. Kolakowski argues that in the end the differences between Trotsky and Lenin on this issue were not that great. Each saw the need to harness the revolutionary potential of the peasantry and each also recognized the potential for antisocialist sentiment within the peasantry and the consequent need for proletarian revolution outside Russia to support the position of the postrevolutionary Russian proletariat.

government also promised the allies--France, England, and the United States--that Russia would remain in the war against Germany.

The February revolution had the support of virtually all strata of the Russian population. In spite of the war and the economic collapse engendered by the war, February was a time of great rejoicing. Throughout Russia voices that had been silenced by tsarist censorship made themselves heard. Newspapers appeared representing every point of view. Political parties, Mensheviks and Bolsheviks among them, now proclaimed their aims in the public press and at public meetings. In St. Petersburg, Moscow, and other large cities, soviets, or councils, were formed that included representatives from workers' and peasants' organizations and representatives from units of the armed forces. Each of the various political parties defended its position within the soviets and pushed for the election of its members to positions of leadership. Within the soviets there was ongoing discussion and debate about the course of the Russian revolution. But the soviets were more than debating societies. With the breakdown of the government and the economic system, the soviets took on a number of governmental powers. For example, they arranged for the distribution of food and fuel to the population of the cities. And the soviets could back their decisions by the disposition of military force. In effect, the soviets formed a system of government alongside the existing government of Kerensky, a system of dual power.

As we have seen, when the war broke out, most Social Democrats abandoned their principles and supported the war efforts of their respective countries. Lenin, in exile in neutral Switzerland, stood by the principles of the Stuttgart resolution, of which he had been one of the authors. He urged the transformation of the war into an international revolutionary war against capitalism. Prevented by the war from traveling to Russia, Lenin could only try to influence the course of events by his writings. In *Imperialism: The Highest Stage of Capitalism* (1915-16), Lenin argued that imperial expansion was necessary for the survival of capitalism and that the war was the outcome of competition between competing capitalist powers. In a series of letters to the editors of the Bolshevik newspaper *Pravda*, he urged revolutionary action. But most of Lenin's letters never appeared in *Pravda*. Within Russia the Bolshevik leadership, including L. B. Kamenev and Stalin, talked of supporting the provisional government of Kerensky and supporting the Russian war effort. They, along with most Social Democrats, saw the February revolution as the bourgeois revolution that marked Russia's transition from feudalism to capitalism. For them, the socialist revolution remained a distant possibility.

Associates in Switzerland approached the German government with a proposal for Lenin and other Bolsheviks to return to Russia across territory controlled by Germany. The German military, hoping that the Bolsheviks would succeed in getting Russia out of the war, agreed. Lenin and other Russian revolutionaries, traveling in a sealed train, arrived in St. Petersburg on April 3, 1917. Within the Bolshevik party Lenin defended a series of theses opposing support for the war and the provisional government and urging the Bolsheviks to support the soviets as the only ruling power within Russia. Mesmerized by the sequential-stages view of history, according to which Russia was slated for a bourgeois revolution, the central committee of the Bolsheviks in St. Petersburg rejected Lenin's position by a vote of thirteen to two.

But Lenin pressed his position. He argued that with the development of the soviets real power had come into the hands of the workers and poor peasants and that it would be a counterrevolutionary step at this point to relinquish power to the provisional government, which supported the interests of the bourgeoisie. Gradually Lenin won over the Bolshevik leadership. The new Bolshevik position struck a responsive chord within the soviets and within Russia as a whole. By July party membership, which had stood at 24,000 in February, had increased to 240,000. In St. Petersburg popular enthusiasm for the revolutionary cause led the Bolsheviks to support a premature uprising that failed. Apparently defeated, Lenin was forced to go into hiding. But by late September, after a failed right-wing military coup, the Bolsheviks had won a majority in the St. Petersburg Soviet, where Lenin's new ally, Leon Trotsky, had been elected president of the Soviet. On October 25 (November 7 on the new calendar), over the continuing objections of some members of the Bolshevik central committee, the Bolsheviks seized power.

The Bolsheviks came to power on the basis of the slogan "bread, peace, and land." Consistent with his early thoughts on the key role of the peasantry, Lenin acted quickly to secure peasant support for Bolshevik rule. On the morning of October 26, the first day of Bolshevik power, the new government abolished private ownership of land but granted the peasants the right to occupy and use the land. In general, the new government proclaimed its socialist principles but did not aim at the immediate socialization of the economy. Instead, it aimed at a mixed economy in which governmental power would lie in the hands of workers and peasants.

Central to the success of the Bolshevik program was the achievement of peace. But Germany demanded a stiff price for peace. In the Brest-Litovsk treaty Russia surrendered a substantial portion of its most productive territory in exchange for peace. But there was no peace. From 1918 to 1920 Russia was torn by civil war. First, Germany, and later other countries, gave its support to several distinct challenges to Bolshevik rule. Independent governments were formed in the Ukraine, Georgia, Siberia, and other areas. Opposition "white" armies were actively supported by some leaders of other political parties, including some Menshevik Marxists. At one time or another seven different foreign powers, including Britain and the United States, sent troops to Russia to support the "whites" in crushing Bolshevism in its cradle. Anti-Bolshevik forces included tsarist generals, supporters of the Kerensky government, and non-Bolshevik revolutionaries, like the anarchist army of Nestor Mahkno in the Ukraine. These "white" forces were not united by a shared political program or by a common command. The civil war was in effect a series of wars with different enemies on different fronts. The Bolshevik-led "red" forces fought back, mobilizing their supporters among the workers and peasants. Terrorist attacks on Lenin, Trotsky, and other Bolshevik leaders were met with "red" terror against their political opponents. As early as December 1917, the Bolsheviks established the Cheka, an internal police force granted extraordinary powers for combatting counterrevolutionary forces. Between 1918 and 1920 the Cheka is thought to have been responsible for the execution of between 12,000 and 50,000 persons. But terror was an instrument of the "white" forces as well. Thousands were brutally executed by both sides.

During this period of "war communism," the central Bolshevik aim was to hold onto power. The Bolsheviks had promised "bread, peace, and land." There was no peace. And there was little bread. The economy, which had begun to fall apart during the tsar's war with Germany, disintegrated even further as the civil war destroyed the means of production and distribution. Bolshevik appeals to the revolutionary ardor of the workers and peasants were supplemented with coercive force. Strikes and demonstrations of workers were suppressed. Peasants were forced at gunpoint to hand over grain and livestock to government representatives. Under such conditions the promise of land meant no more than the promises of peace and bread. In spite of all of this, and in spite of the death of many of their most class-conscious supporters in the civil war, the Bolsheviks prevailed.[6]

---

6.   The 1928 novel *And Quiet Flows the Don* by Mikhail Sholokhov (New York: Vintage, 1966) provides a rich and panoramic view of the revolutionary struggle throughout the civil war. See also the novel by Nikolai Ostovsky, *How The Steel Was Tempered* (1932-1933) (Moscow: Progress, n.d.).

By late 1920 the civil war was effectively over. But the Bolsheviks faced an economy in ruins. Thousands of refugees were without food or shelter. Famine spread. The supporting socialist revolutions in other countries, which Bolsheviks had hoped would be sparked by the Russian example, had failed to materialize, in spite of the best efforts of the Bolshevik-organized Third International. Within Russia the Bolsheviks faced a peasantry seething with discontent at the policies of war communism. Strikes against the deplorable conditions of workers broke out, sometimes raising political demands in opposition to the Bolsheviks. In March 1921, sailors at the Kronstadt garrison, heroes of the October revolution, rebelled in defense of the workers and peasants from whose ranks they had come. They demanded free markets for agricultural products and an end to forced requisitions of grain. Because of the strong support that opposition political parties, particularly anarchists, found at Kronstadt, the Bolsheviks used force to crush the sailors.[7]

If these difficulties were not enough, a fundamental challenge to Bolshevik policies was mounted by forces within the party. The Workers' Opposition--led by A. G. Shlyapnikov, A. A. Bogdanov, and Alexandra Kollontai--charged the Bolshevik leadership with deviating from the path of true Marxism. It called for a radical change in the economy in which power over economic decision making would be taken from the bureaucracies and handed over to the workers themselves. In addition, it called for greater freedom, openness, and democracy within the party and government institutions.[8] If instituted, these policies would have resulted, in fact, in abdication of Bolshevik rule.

Lenin responded to the external discontent and internal opposition with two steps that were to have lasting significance for the communist movement. First, considering internal opposition under the existing difficult circumstances a threat to the survival of the revolution, Lenin persuaded the Bolshevik party to accept a ban on all internal factions. Second, overcoming strong opposition within the party, he instituted a fundamental change in economic policy. The New Economic Policy (NEP) marked a turn away from war communism back to the mixed

---

7. Suppression of the Kronstadt mutiny was the final straw that broke the support of the American anarchist Emma Goldman for the revolution. Goldman, who was in Russia at the time, gives her comments on the significance of this event in Emma Goldman, *Living My Life*, vol. 2 (New York: Dover, 1970), pp. 884-888. Compare also Alexander Berkman, *The Russian Tragedy* (Sanday: Cienfuegos Press, 1976), pp. 69-108.

8. See "The Workers' Opposition" by Alexandra Kollontai in Alexandra Kollontai, *Selected Writings*, ed. Alix Holt (New York: W. W. Norton, 1977), pp. 159-200.

economy envisaged in the early days of the October revolution. In particular, the NEP put an end to forced requisition of grain and allowed for free markets in agricultural produce and many other goods. It also allowed for greater reliance on and higher pay for technical and managerial specialists. Public ownership and control remained only for the "commanding heights" of the economy: banking, transport, communications, and the like. Lenin called this system "state capitalism." Lenin had himself earlier opposed free markets in grain as, in a country largely made up of peasants, tantamount to the abandonment of socialism.[9] In 1921 he supported it as a necessary retreat from the policies of war communism. Even then it was opposed by some Bolsheviks who saw it as a betrayal of socialism. On January 21, 1924, after a series of debilitating strokes, Lenin died. He left the task of constructing a genuinely socialist system to those who would come after him. In the next chapter we will examine the attempt to build such a fully socialist system in the USSR.

---

9.   Kolakowski, *Main Currents*, vol. 2, pp. 482-483.

6

The Soviet Model

The war and the Bolshevik revolution caused a split in the international socialist movement. As we have seen, initially most of the European social democratic parties supported the war effort of their respective countries. As the war went on, social democratic opposition to the war grew stronger. Three camps developed within the social democratic movement: patriotic support for the war effort, pacifistic demand for an end to all hostilities, and call for transformation of the war into revolutionary war. Lenin was one of the leaders of the revolutionary camp. The Bolshevik revolution was a successful application of this revolutionary strategy. But it was also built upon the new type of party that Lenin had advocated as far back as 1902--a party made up of dedicated revolutionaries organized according to the principles of "democratic centralism" that subordinated all party members to the control of the elected central leadership. In the years following the Bolshevik revolution, this new type of party, which Lenin had championed in 1902 only as necessary under backward Russian conditions, came to be seen by Lenin and his followers as universally necessary for genuinely revolutionary socialism.

The failure of the social democratic parties in the advanced Western countries to resist the war or take advantage of the revolutionary opportunity presented by the war convinced Lenin that these parties were hopelessly corrupted. Their leadership was opportunistic, more interested in preserving its own niche in the social order than in changing it. Their membership was to a significant degree co-opted by higher wages and welfare benefits paid for by wealth extracted from the colonized people of Africa, Asia, and Latin America. And their party press and party intellectuals were contaminated with bourgeois ideology.[1]

Convinced that the Second International was corrupted by counterrevolutionary ideology and counterrevolutionary leadership, the Bolsheviks moved, in March of 1919 during the height of the civil war, to organize a new "communist" international. The aim of this Third International was to apply the lessons of the Russian revolution on an international scale. In founding it, the Bolsheviks hoped to draw the truly revolutionary elements out of the moribund institutions of the Second International and to set them on a course of action that would further the cause of international proletarian revolution. But enthusiasm for the Bolshevik revolution exceeded understanding of the principles it embodied, and many of those who were attracted to the First Congress of the new International were not sufficiently revolutionary in Bolshevik eyes. Accordingly, at the Second Congress of the Third International in Moscow in 1920, the Bolsheviks laid down twenty-one conditions that were to be required of all parties affiliated with the new International. Among these twenty-one conditions were requirements for the organization of affiliated parties along the lines of the party of the new type advocated by Lenin in 1902. In particular, the conditions required application of the principle of democratic centralism, control of all party press by the central committee of the party, central control of all party factions and expulsion of all groups resistant to such central control, support for the dictatorship of the proletariat, and creation of an apparatus capable of continuing the activities of the party in the event that party activity was made illegal. In addition, the twenty-one conditions called for affiliated parties to identify themselves as "communist" in order to distinguish themselves from the "social democratic" and "socialist" parties of the Second International.[2] In this

---

1.   Prior to the war, as for example in his *Marxism and Revisionism* (1908) in V. I. Lenin, *Against Revisionism* (Moscow: Progress, 1976), Lenin had criticized elements within the Second International for their capitulation to bourgeois philosophy and their consequent antirevolutionary reformism. In *Imperialism, the Highest Stage of Capitalism* (1915-1916) (Moscow: Progress, 1975), pp. 116-117, he developed the idea of a labor aristocracy in the advanced economies that had been bought off by capitalism. After the Bolshevik revolution and the clear failure of the revolution in other countries, Lenin came to see the rottenness of the Second International as more pervasive than he had earlier realized. See, for example, *The Proletarian Revolution and the Renegade Kautsky* (1918) and *Our Revolution* (1923), in Lenin, *Against Revisionism*.

2.   For the full text of the twenty-one conditions, see Helmut Gruber, ed., *International Communism in the Era of Lenin: A Documentary History* (Garden City: Anchor, 1972), pp. 241-246.

way, the Third International aimed at splitting the Second International and organizing its revolutionary elements into a new international grouping.

In general, the Bolsheviks were successful in splitting the social democratic parties in nearly every country, though it cannot be said that the resulting "communist" parties always truly satisfied the twenty-one conditions.[3] Nonetheless, after 1920 the words "communist" and "socialist" take on clearly distinct meanings that they did not have before. Before the Bolshevik revolution Marxists tended to use the terms "socialism" and "communism" in more or less interchangeable ways. In fact, they were more likely to use the term "social democracy" than either of the others. To be sure, in *Critique of the Gotha Program*, written in 1875, Marx wrote that "between capitalist and communist society lies the period of the revolutionary transformation of the one into the other." But Marx does not call this transition period "socialism." Instead, he called it the "revolutionary dictatorship of the proletariat."[4] Elsewhere in the same text Marx distinguished between the "first phase of communist society as it is when it has just emerged after prolonged birth pangs from capitalist society" and a "higher phase of communist society."[5] But again, the term "socialism" did not appear. Later Soviet thinkers did employ the terms "socialism" and "communism" to identify distinct stages in the development of postcapitalist societies, but this particular terminological distinction is not rooted in classical Marxism and does not capture the important political difference between "communist" and "socialist" political parties.

The historically significant difference between "communist" and "socialist" is this. In 1920 the worldwide Marxist movement split into two camps: communists who adopted the ideas of Lenin and joined parties affiliated with the Third International, and socialists who rejected the ideas of Lenin and remained outside the Third International. To be sure, there were and are self-proclaimed "socialists" who are not Marxists. And of course, socialists and communists each maintain that the other is not truly Marxist. But it is the split in the international Marxist movement into competing "socialist" and "communist" movements that is historically important.

---

3. Adam Westoby, *The Evolution of Communism* (New York: Free Press, 1989), pp. 47-52.

4. Karl Marx, *Critique of the Gotha Program* (1875) (Moscow: Progress, 1971), p. 26.

5. Ibid., pp. 17-18.

From very early on, many Marxists denounced the Bolshevik revolution as a perversion of Marxism. Among them was Karl Kautsky, the leading theoretician of the Second International. One week after the Bolshevik seizure of power, Kautsky wrote an article in which he stressed the difficulties facing a workers' party in power in overwhelmingly agrarian Russia. He argued that under such circumstances the working class should not attempt to implement socialism, but should instead work for a democratic, parliamentary republic.[6]

In fact, elections for a parliamentary body, the Constituent Assembly, had been planned before the October revolution for the end of November 1917. The elections did take place as scheduled. The Bolsheviks won about 25 percent of the vote. Mensheviks won only 4 percent. And bourgeois parties won about 13 percent. The strongest electoral showing was by the Socialist Revolutionary Party (SRs), which, though it claimed to represent the peasants, was in fact divided between a hesitant left wing, which for a while cooperated with the Bolsheviks, and a right wing, represented by Kerensky, which intended no immediate fundamental social change and no end to the war. The moderate socialists in the pre-Bolshevik provisional government, Mensheviks, Socialist Revolutionaries and independents like Kerensky held the view that historical development followed a definite sequence of stages according to which a period of capitalism must precede the dawn of socialism. Accordingly, they expected a period of capitalism to follow the overthrow of the "feudal" tsarist regime. These moderate socialists were also committed to the principles of democratic electoral politics. They saw their task as one of cooperation with the liberal procapitalist parties, like the Cadets, against reactionary opponents. From this point of view the time was not ripe for further revolutionary changes.[7]

To be sure, the strong support for the Socialist Revolutionaries from the countryside rested on the SRs' advocacy of programs of land reform, which would have taken land from the large landowners and divided it among the peasants. But fearing to alienate their allies among the bourgeoisie, the moderate SRs in the provisional government did not immediately move to implement this land-reform program. It was the moderate SRs who would have been the dominant group in the elected

---

6. Massimo Salvadori, *Karl Kautsky and the Socialist Revolution 1880-1938* (London: NLB, 1979), pp. 223-225.

7. Mikhail Heller and Aleksandr Nekrich, *Utopia in Power* (New York: Summit Books, 1986), p. 31.

constituent assembly. To follow the advice of Kautsky and other moderate socialists would have required the Bolsheviks to relinquish power to these SRs and their allies among the bourgeois parties. In Lenin's view this would have resulted in the preservation of Russian capitalism. It would have annulled the hopes for an end to the war and for redistribution of land in the countryside. This Lenin and the Bolsheviks refused to do. Lenin argued that it would be a great mistake to adhere rigidly to the forms of parliamentary democracy and abandon the "democratic" substance of the revolution in process.[8] Accordingly, the Bolsheviks ordered armed sailors to disperse the assembly when it convened in January of 1918 and to fire on peaceful demonstrations of workers in support of the assembly.[9] In place of parliamentary democracy Lenin and the Bolsheviks proclaimed the dictatorship of the proletariat. This was a step of great importance for defining the nature of the Soviet regime that would be built on the foundation of the Bolshevik revolution. It would not be a democratic republic.

At this point Kautsky turned from guarded support for the Bolshevik revolution to outright hostility. In *Democracy or Dictatorship?* and *The Dictatorship of the Proletariat*, both written in 1918, Kautsky criticized the Bolsheviks for their betrayal of democracy and consequently also their betrayal of socialism, since, in Kautsky's view, there could be no socialism without democracy. In these works and a whole series of works that followed, Kautsky led an ideological crusade against the Bolsheviks in which he argued that the outcome of the Bolshevik revolution was not socialism but a new tyranny in which it is the so-called communists who exploit the workers and in which--in the absence of democracy, freedom of press, and freedom of organization--the workers are incapable of resistance.[10]

Kautsky was not alone among Marxists in raising such criticisms. Within Russia itself Marxists spoke out against the course of the Russian revolution. Plekhanov, the father of Russian Marxism, recalled Engels's fears of a premature seizure of power and denounced the dictatorship of the Bolsheviks as the dictatorship of a group supported by terroristic means having nothing to do with Marxism or socialism.[11] Vera

---

8. See Leszek Kolakowski, *Main Currents of Marxism*, vol. 2 (Oxford: Clarendon Press, 1978), p. 480-481.

9. Heller and Nekrich, *Utopia in Power*, pp. 48-49.

10. Salvadori, *Karl Kautsky*, pp. 251-293.

11. Jane Burbank, *Intelligentsia and Revolution* (Oxford: Oxford University Press, 1986), p. 36.

Zasulich, along with Plekhanov one of the founders of the Russian Social Democratic Labor Party, a woman who had corresponded with Marx and Engels, denounced the Bolshevik revolution as a counterrevolutionary coup.[12] Pavel Axelrod, another of the founders of the Russian Social Democratic Labor Party, called on European socialists and workers to take action against the Bolsheviks.[13] And Iulii Martov, long one of the leading theoreticians of Russian Marxism, saw the Bolshevik attempt as hopelessly at odds with Marxist theory of history and, in its resort to violent force, fundamentally at odds with Marxist cultural values.[14]

Even Rosa Luxemburg, who sided with Lenin in urging the transformation of the war into a revolutionary war and who became one of the founders of the Communist movement in Germany, expressed strong reservations about what was happening in Russia. Imprisoned by the German government during the war, Luxemburg composed her thoughts on what was happening in Russia on the basis of the bits of information that reached her and on the basis of her own years of experience in the social democratic movement. In prison in 1918, during the first year of Bolshevik rule, she wrote:

> In place of the representative bodies created by general, popular elections, Lenin and Trotsky have laid down the soviets as the only true representation of the laboring masses. But with the repression of political life in the land as a whole, life in the soviets must also become more and more crippled. Without general elections, without unrestricted freedom of press and assembly, without a free struggle of opinion, life dies out in every public institution, becomes a mere semblance of life, in which only the bureaucracy remains as the active element. Public life gradually falls asleep, a few dozen party leaders of inexhaustible energy and boundless experience direct and rule. Among them, in reality only a dozen outstanding heads do the leading and an elite of the working class is invited from time to time to meetings where they are to applaud the speeches of the leaders, and to approve proposed resolutions unanimously --at bottom, then, a clique affair . . . [which] must inevitably cause a brutalization of public life.[15]

---

12. Ibid., p. 44.
13. Ibid., p. 50.
14. Ibid., pp. 19-27.
15. Rosa Luxemburg, *The Russian Revolution* (Ann Arbor: University of Michigan Press, 1977), pp. 71-72.

This prescient criticism, made public at a time when enthusiasm for the Bolsheviks was sweeping much of the socialist movement including many of Luxemburg's friends and supporters, points to the true absence of democracy as a fatal flaw in Bolshevism.

Nonetheless, Luxemburg tried to maintain critical support for the revolutionary Marxism of the Bolsheviks. Released from prison after the overthrow of Kaiser Wilhelm, she took her place as one of the leaders of the Spartacus League at the revolutionary end of the spectrum of German Marxism. Shortly before she was murdered, she spoke at the founding convention of the German Communist Party.[16] And even more than Luxemburg, many Marxists, in many different countries, saw in Russian communism a revolutionary way out of the quagmire of social democratic parliamentarianism, which had proven itself so unprincipled and so ineffective.

Further, many Marxists agreed with the Bolsheviks that their methods were in fact more "democratic" than a rigid adherence to the forms of parliamentary democracy. Was it realistic to expect that illiterate Russian peasants, without experience of electoral politics and without a true knowledge of the hollowness of SR promises of radical change, could vote in their own best interests? The simple truth is that the Bolsheviks could not have prevailed against the forces arrayed against them had they not had the strong support of both the workers and peasants, the masses of ordinary people. During World War I, 10 million workers and peasants in Russia were under arms. Lenin attributed the victory of the Bolsheviks to the fact that the Bolsheviks ended the war and gave land to the peasants.[17]   These steps were profoundly democratic. It is unlikely that either would have been achieved by the elected constituent assembly. Nor arguably, could they have been achieved without the rough methods of the Bolsheviks. Land and peace threatened vested interests. These interests fought back with violent force and could be expected to take advantage of every opportunity that presented itself to regain what had been lost. A. S. Martynov, a Menshevik opponent of Lenin, retired from politics to become an engineer in the Ukraine during the early days after the Bolshevik October. Witnessing there the bloody conflicts that ensued between the various contending forces, Martynov drew the conclusion, one with

---

16.   Rosa Luxemburg, "Speech to the Founding Convention of the German Communist Party," in Mary-Alice Waters, ed., *Rosa Luxemburg Speaks* (New York: Pathfinder, 1990), pp. 400-427. On Luxemburg's relationship to the Bolsheviks, see Waters' introduction, pp. 24-30.

17.   Leszek Kolakowski, *Main Currents*, p. 481.

which the historian Roy Medvedev agreed, that only the Bolshevik dictatorship could save the situation.[18]

One might argue that the civil war and the collapse of the economy could have been avoided in the first place if the Bolsheviks had refrained from precipitous action and allowed the elected government to take power. But it is not clear that this is so. The SRs appear to have been committed to continuing the war. And under the leadership of Kerensky the provisional government showed no intention of actually implementing the SRs' promised agrarian reforms. On both of these key issues, pressures from below were fundamentally at odds with what would have been governmental policy. In short, there were forces at work in Russian society that necessitated radical change--change that by its nature and by the backwardness of Russian political institutions was almost certain to produce violent confrontation.

On October 25, one day after seizing power, the Bolsheviks made public a decree on peace and a decree on land. The decree on peace called for an immediate armistice. The decree on land proclaimed the confiscation of all land as the property of the whole people but granted to the peasants the rights to occupy and use the land. The text of the decree on land followed the exact wording of a program drawn up by an SR newspaper. An SR delegate to the Second Congress of Soviets chided Lenin for compromising his supposed "Marxist" opposition to small private agriculture: "'A fine Marxist this is,' they said, 'who has harassed us for fifteen years from the heights of his Marxist grandeur . . . but who no sooner seizes power than he implements our program.'" To this Lenin replied: "A fine party it is which had to be driven from power before its program could be implemented."[19] These two measures, ending the war and allowing peasants to use the land, were extremely popular. They gained the Bolsheviks a great deal of support that was of critical importance in the early part of the civil war that followed.

The Bolshevik example inspired revolutionary socialists in many different countries. In each case, war-weary soldiers and sailors joined with workers to form workers' councils modeled on the Russian soviets. These workers' councils provided activists who were recruited for revolutionary attempts. In Berlin the Spartacus League attempted an armed uprising in January 1919. The attempt was defeated, and the

---

18. Roy Medvedev, *Leninism and Western Socialism* (London: Verso, 1981), p. 36 (Martynov), and p. 35 (Medvedev).

19. Quoted in Heller and Nekrich, *Utopia in Power*, p. 44. On the provisional government's procrastination on land reform, see Medvedev, *Leninism*, p. 103.

Spartacus leaders, Rosa Luxemburg and Karl Liebknecht, were murdered. The same year a similarly Bolshevik-inspired attempt in Bavaria was put down by force. In Hungary a Communist Republic briefly stood from March to July 1919 before it was savagely repressed with the help of "Western allies." Other attempts in central Germany in 1921 and 1923 also failed. Although the Russian experience had inspired the creation of Communist parties in most of the European countries, in the United States, and in other parts of the world, by the time of Lenin's death in January 1924 it was clear to all that for the foreseeable future, at least, Soviet Russia stood alone.

During the 1920s, under the NEP, the Soviet economy began to recover from the devastations of war and civil war. By 1927 production had returned to prewar levels, and efforts were under way to build the foundations for a modern industrial economy. The Soviet economy during the time of the NEP operated on the basis of a mixture of self-interest, socialist idealism, and patriotic pride. Granted the rights to occupation and use of the land within a system of relatively free markets, the Russian peasants responded with the hard work and shrewd business sense of small farmers everywhere. Throughout the Soviet economy private entrepreneurs, the so-called NEP men, responded to opportunities for profit offered by the market. Fortunes were made and sometimes squandered.

But other forces were at work as well. Inspired with the dream of building socialism, thousands of young people volunteered for hard work in the countryside, mines, factories, and frontiers of the Soviet Union. Political activists, drawn into action during the revolution and civil war, now struggled with the tasks of economic construction through their local and regional Party organizations. Thousands of skilled foreign workers migrated to the Soviet Union, eager to be a part of what was happening there. And each new power plant, each new tractor, each new locomotive carried with it feelings of pride in what the new Soviet society had accomplished.[20]

The decade of the 1920s was also a time of many different cultural currents. The avant garde art of the Russian formalists, which flowered in the first decade of the twentieth century, continued to make its presence felt in postrevolutionary culture as well. Sympathetic to the Bolshevik cause, many of these artists had helped to create a

---

20. Ilya Ilf and Eugene Petrov offer a comic view of the NEP period with its mixture of greed and idealism in their 1928 novel, *The Little Golden Calf* (New York: Frederick Ungar, 1961).

revolutionary art that went beyond the bounds of bourgeois sensibility. In the 1920s this formalist current continued. Artists hoped to use the visual arts, theater, and literature to deepen and reenforce revolutionary consciousness. Often supportive of revolutionary values, they were also sharply critical of the burgeoning bureaucracies and the backward thinking of soviet officials and ordinary people.[21]

Although all organized political opposition to Communist Party rule was suppressed, the 1920s was a time in which there was relative freedom in Soviet culture. The avant garde art of the Russian formalists and their descendants continued to find a public stage in spite of the fact that most Communist Party functionaries (Lenin included) detested it. Numerous artists and intellectuals traveled outside the Soviet Union. Conflicting points of view appeared in the press and in other cultural arenas, even though these arenas were regulated by government censorship. Philosophers who were sharply critical of Lenin's position were appointed to top positions in academic institutions and government service.[22] Academic institutions retained a degree of independence. Darwinian evolutionary theories and relativistic physics, which would later be banned from Soviet science, were debated in Soviet academic and research institutions just as they were in much of the rest of the world.[23]

From a political point of view the Soviet Union faced an uncertain future. With no supporting socialist revolution elsewhere in the world, the Soviet experiment had to proceed in a hostile international environment, without external material, intellectual, or spiritual assistance. The classical Marxist vision of socialism as a planned economy arising out of advanced industrial capitalism offered little help to Soviet Communists faced with a largely preindustrial economy. NEP had been adopted out of necessity. But where should the Soviet experiment go from there?

Nikolai Bukharin, whom Lenin once identified as "the favorite of the whole [Bolshevik] Party," in spite of the fact that, in Lenin's view, "his

---

21. V. V. Mayakovsky's plays are perhaps archetypical of this period. In *Mystery-Bouffe* (1918) he strongly endorsed the revolution. In *The Bedbug* (1928) and *The Bathhouse* (1929) he was sharply critical of Soviet bureaucracy and Soviet officials. In 1930 Mayakovsky committed suicide.

22. Richard Hudelson, *Marxism and Philosophy in the Twentieth Century* (New York: Praeger, 1990), pp. 43-44.

23. On Soviet science, see David Joravsky, *Soviet Marxism and Natural Science* (New York: Columbia University, 1961); and Loren Graham, *Science and Philosophy in the Soviet Union* (New York: Knopf, 1972).

theoretical views can be classified as fully Marxist only with great reserve," argued for a continuation of the policy of the NEP.[24] Bukharin held that such a policy, coupled with a gradually expanding state sector and Communist direction of the economy as a whole, would eventually lead to socialism. Opposing this policy was a coalition within the ruling Communist Party that came to be known as the "left opposition." Led by Leon Trotsky and Evgenii Preobrazhenskii, the left opposition argued that a change in direction was necessary, both as a step toward the industrialization required by socialism and in order to block the development of a political opposition.

Marxists had always thought of socialism as coming after the industrial development achieved by capitalism. The planned use of economic resources for the satisfaction of human needs and for the free development of every individual presupposed the existence of productive resources adequate for such purposes. In the Soviet Union such resources were lacking. Preobrazhenskii argued that the only way to build such resources in the Soviet Union was by extracting savings from the peasant sector of the economy. This was to be accomplished by charging higher than market prices for goods produced by the state-controlled industrial sector for goods sold to the peasants and by keeping prices for agricultural goods depressed.

This left policy meant an abandonment of free markets. But in 1925 the Communist Party moved in the opposite direction, relaxing state fixing of grain prices, reducing agricultural taxes, extending the lease periods on land, and even permitting prosperous farmers to hire wage laborers to work for them. From the opposition point of view, these policies not only prevented the accumulation of capital necessary for increased industrialization, they also helped create a potential political opposition. Here the position of the left touches on issues raised in the prerevolutionary period. Recall that in the years before the revolution Trotsky had opposed the idea of a government of workers and peasants on the grounds that, as small proprietors, the peasants were by nature hostile to socialism. Now, Trotsky and Preobrazhenskii argued, the present policies were fostering the growth of just such a class of

---

24. Lenin characterization of Bukharin comes from a document known as "Lenin's Testament" written in December 1922 and January 1923. See "Letter to the Congress," in Robert Tucker, ed., *The Lenin Anthology* (New York: Norton, 1975), p. 727. Stephen Cohen, *Rethinking the Soviet Experience: Politics and History Since 1917* (New York: Oxford University Press, 1985), p. 60, says that near the end of his life Lenin developed a defense of the NEP as a road to socialism. Silviu Brucan, *The Post-Brezhnev Era* (New York: Praeger, 1983), p. 16, claims that there was some inconsistency in Lenin's thinking on this point.

independent farmers who would have both an interest in resisting socialism and the economic power to do so. From this point of view, Bukharin's expectation that somehow the NEP would evolve into socialism rested on nothing more than blind faith. Bukharin, however, viewed any attempt to renege on the NEP bargain struck with the peasantry as politically dangerous and morally unacceptable. Such a move would be politically dangerous because it would risk alienating the masses of peasants. It was, after all, because of discontent among the peasantry, that NEP had been adopted in the first place.[25]

These differences over the future course of Soviet society became entangled with an internal struggle for power within the Communist Party of the Soviet Union in the years following the death of Lenin. Leon Trotsky was the obvious successor to Lenin. One of the leaders of the 1905 revolutionary movement, Trotsky stood as an independent socialist, affiliated neither with the Bolsheviks nor the Mensheviks in the years between 1905 and 1917. Although sometimes critical of Lenin and the Leninist conception of the party, Trotsky joined with Lenin in spring and summer 1917 in trying to push the Bolsheviks beyond support for the bourgeois revolution toward independent revolutionary action. Trotsky's election as president of the St. Petersburg soviet in late September 1917 indicated both strong support for the Bolsheviks and Trotsky's own popularity with the workers and soldiers who formed the grass-roots foundation for the Bolshevik revolution. In the years of struggle that followed Trotsky served on the central committee of the Bolshevik Party and as the commissar in charge of the military aspects of the civil war. A recognized figure in the international movement prior to the Russian revolution, in the course of the revolution and civil war, Trotsky acquired fame second only to Lenin as a revolutionary leader. Trotsky was Lenin's heir apparent.[26]

But Trotsky faced opposition within the party. In part this opposition went back to the prerevolutionary period in which Trotsky had stood as an opponent of the Bolsheviks. In part, too, opposition to Trotsky rested on apprehension concerning the arrogance and style of leadership he exhibited in the course of the revolutionary period. In part, also, opposition to Trotsky grew out of fears that his strong leadership would be used to change the direction of policy away from the NEP. And in

---

25. Stephen Cohen, *Bukharin and the Bolshevik Revolution* (Oxford: Oxford University Press, 1980), pp. 160-201, provides a view of these debates within the Soviet Union.

26. In his "Testament," p. 727, Lenin identifies Trotsky as "perhaps the most capable man" on the Bolshevik Central Committee.

part, opposition to Trotsky grew out of the personal ambitions of his opponents within the party. In any event, an alliance between Joseph Stalin, Grigori Zinoviev, L. B. Kamenev, and Nikolai Bukharin, all old Bolsheviks and members of the Bolshevik central committee, succeeded in blocking Trotsky's ascension to leadership. In this way a split developed within the Bolshevik party between the left opposition led by Trotsky and the group in control of the party leadership. Lenin had foreseen the possibility of this split and had taken steps to prevent it but to no avail.[27]

Gradually, in the mid-1920s, the left opposition was isolated and removed from positions of influence within the party. By 1928 Trotsky was forced into exile. But now, under the leadership of Stalin, a campaign was launched within the party against the "right" wing of the party led by Bukharin. At a meeting of the party central committee in July 1928, Stalin endorsed the program of the left that he had heretofore strongly opposed. The time had come, he said, to halt the growing strength of the kulaks, the prosperous peasants, and to initiate a process of rapid industrialization. Bukharin and other supporters of the NEP, in particular A. Rykov, the Soviet premier, and Mikhail Tomsky, who was head of the trade unions, led an opposition to this proposed change of course. But having used his position as Party secretary to place his own supporters in positions of power, Stalin was successful in defeating this opposition. By the end of 1929 Bukharin and his followers had been driven from their posts within the government and party bureaucracies. Stalin had managed to gain individual control over the party.

More important for the fate of millions of human beings and for the future development of communism was the decision taken by Stalin in late 1929 to embark on a policy of collectivization of Soviet agriculture. This policy had two aims. On the one hand, it was hoped that by organizing agriculture into large collective farms it would be possible to utilize heavy machinery in place of human labor, freeing human labor for the tasks of building up the industrial infrastructure of the Soviet Union. On the other hand, by doing away with small independent farms, the Communist Party would prevent the formation of a political opposition based on a class of small proprietors. These aims were, of

---

27. In December 1922, in bad health and fearing a split within the party, Lenin dictated a document commonly referred to as "Lenin's Testament" in which he commented on the persons in the central leadership positions and called for the removal of Stalin from his position as party secretary. This document is reprinted in Tucker, *The Lenin Anthology*, pp. 725-727. On p. xxiii Tucker mentions a report on the Thirteenth Party Conference that showed signs of the coming split.

course, the very aims that motivated the left opposition of Trotsky and Preobrazhenskii. But the means Stalin employed in achieving them went beyond anything previously imagined. By the coercion of armed force the peasants were herded onto the collective farms. Many peasants resisted. They destroyed grain supplies and slaughtered livestock in order to prevent their falling into the hands of the central authorities. Armed revolts in some villages were violently suppressed. Peasants were denied the internal passports now required for movement within the Soviet Union. Millions of peasants identified as well-to-do kulaks, were deported to labor camps in Siberia and other parts of the Soviet Union. One Soviet writer described the forced expulsion of kulaks from a village:

> From our village . . . the "kulaks" were driven out on foot. They took what they could carry on their backs: bedding, clothing. The mud was so deep it pulled the boots off their feet. It was terrible to watch them. They marched along in a column and looked back at their huts, and their bodies still held the warmth from their own stoves. What pain they must have suffered! After all, they had been born in those houses; they had given their daughters in marriage in those cabins. They had heated up their stoves, and the cabbage soup they had cooked was left there behind them. The milk had not been drunk, and smoke was still rising from their chimneys. The women were sobbing--but were afraid to scream. The Party activists didn't give a damn about them. We drove them off like geese.[28]

Very many of these deported peasants died in labor camps. The remaining peasants were forced onto collective farms, which typically lacked adequate housing, water, or sewage facilities and from which government officials confiscated most or even all that was produced. Lacking any incentive to produce and facing shortages of food, agricultural workers consumed what little food and animal stocks remained. Millions died of starvation.[29]

The collectivization of agriculture was the centerpiece for a new direction in policy adopted in 1929. Another giant step taken at this time was the implementation of an economic system that extended government planning and control to cover all aspects of the economy. Those private enterprises that had been tolerated during the period of

---

28. Quoted in Robert Conquest, *The Harvest of Sorrow* (New York: Oxford University Press, 1986), p. 137.

29. Conquest *Harvest of Sorrow*, p. 306, estimates the total death toll among the peasants as a result of dekulakization and famine to be about 14.5 million human beings.

the NEP were eliminated. Government bureaucracies decided what was to be produced by whom and worked out a detailed plan that stipulated for each enterprise what and how much it should produce, where its inputs would come from, and to whom it should deliver its final products. This was the first Five-Year Plan. Through its control of the government and the planning bureaucracies, the Communist Party at this time gained complete control of the economic life of the Soviet Union.

In addition, during this period the Communist Party claimed control over all aspects of Soviet cultural life. Non-Marxist academics were driven from their positions in the universities and research institutions. Communist Party positions dictated what could be done in the arts. Formalism and other avant garde art forms, which had continued to appear throughout the 1920s, were no longer tolerated. Communist Party decisions determined what could and what could not be said in philosophy. And in science, party positions ruled against Einstein's relativity theory and Darwinian evolutionary theory.[30]

In foreign policy, the first Five-Year Plan, based on the expectation of a coming crisis of capitalism, called on Communists around the world to prepare for a time of revolutionary opportunity by sharply distinguishing themselves and their revolutionary intent from the Social Democrats and other reformist parties. Occurring as it did during a time of polarization and the rise of fascism within European politics, this Communist policy significantly weakened the European left.

An underlying theme supporting these policies was one of revolutionary self-reliance. Stalin called on members of the party and the Soviet people to renew themselves to the cause of socialism. The heroic struggle of the revolution and civil war had not been fought to make the kulaks rich, he said. The NEP had been forced on the Russian revolution as a necessary retreat. The "left deviationists" maintained that socialism could not be won in the Soviet Union in the absence of revolution in the West. The "right deviationists" feared the prosperous

---

30. On the history of Soviet Science, see Joravsky, *Soviet Marxism*, and Graham, Science and Philosophy. For a general overview of the period from 1929 to 1934, see Mikhail Heller and Aleksandr Nekrich, *Utopia in Power*, "The Great Rupture," pp. 222-276. Heller and Nekrich argue that the evils of "Stalinism" shaped during this period were inherent in the Bolshevik revolution from the beginning. Galina Vishnevskaya's *Galina* (San Diego: Harcourt Brace Jovanovich, 1984), an autobiographical account by a major Russian opera singer, provides a picture from the post-World War II period of the corrupting and demoralizing influence of Communist Party control of this important Russian art form.

peasants. Against both of these, Stalin maintained that socialism could be built in one country and that the Communist Party of the Soviet Union, if only it had the will for heroic struggle, could lead Soviet workers and poor peasants in this great undertaking. Communists must rise to the historical task at hand. This spirit, working alongside careerist aspirations for advancement, drew young party members into the campaign for collectivization of agriculture and into the drive for rapid industrialization that accompanied it.[31]

By the end of the first Five-Year Plan the collectivization of agriculture was complete but only at the cost of enormous human suffering. Significant strides had been made in industrialization, but even here there were evident failures involving great waste of precious resources. In the second Five-Year Plan, which covered the years from 1934 to 1939, Stalin admitted to certain "excesses" in the collectivization of agriculture and problems in the process of industrialization. He blamed these difficulties on enemies of socialism outside and inside the Communist Party. In the years that followed, the Stalinist leadership purged the party of all who posed any potential political challenge to Stalin. Accused of being saboteurs, wreckers, or traitors to Soviet communism, thousands of "old Bolsheviks" were expelled from the party and either sent to labor camps in Siberia or killed. By 1939 virtually all those who had been in the party at the time of the revolution, and especially those who had held positions of leadership within the Party, had been expelled.[32] The dictatorship of the proletariat had passed from the dictatorship of the Communist Party to the dictatorship of a single individual.

By the end of the 1930s the basic features of the Soviet system that would prevail for nearly fifty years were in place. The mixed economy of the NEP had been replaced by a comprehensive centrally planned economy, and the fundamental monopoly on political power, which had been held by the Communist Party ever since the time of the October revolution, had been extended into a system of Communist control of all aspects of cultural life. In these essentials the Soviet system would serve as the model for the communist systems developed in Eastern Europe, Asia, and other parts of the world after World War II. Although in Eastern Europe this Soviet model was, with few exceptions, imposed by

---

31. In *Children of the Arbat* by Anatoli Rybakov (New York: Dell, 1988), we gain a picture not only of the degradation and despair that came to the members of this generation of Soviets but also of the idealism of their youth.

32. For an account of the trial and execution of Bukharin, see S. Cohen, *Bukharin*, pp. 372-381.

Soviet military power, in other parts of the world, particularly those that had struggled to free themselves from the colonial domination of the Western capitalist powers, the Soviet system was seen as an attractive model for economic development and political independence. In the next chapter we will consider the spread of Soviet-style communism to other parts of the world.

7

International Communism

Marx's *Capital* considers the fate of a capitalistically organized social system as it develops over time in isolation from external interaction with other social systems. As Marx was well aware, this isolation was a theoretically useful simplification that would have to be suspended in any analysis of particular actual social systems.[1] One of the more fruitful theoretical developments of the period of the Second International was the effort to understand capitalist systems in the context of the more complex economic and political structures so characteristic of late nineteenth-century imperialism.[2]

The theory of imperialism was important in several respects. First, imperialism was clearly a development of major importance that Marxism, as social theory, needed to address.

Second, the theory of imperialism provided a way to reconcile classical Marxism with some apparently recalcitrant facts. Marxism predicted the polarization of classes and the disappearance of the middle classes, but in fact the middle classes persisted. Marxism predicted (in at least some interpretations) that workers' wages would hover at subsistence levels, but in fact a significant number of workers in the major capitalist countries were enjoying a gradually growing standard of living. Marxism predicted falling rates of profit, but in fact rates of profit remained fairly stable. And Marxism predicted crises of increased frequency and depth, whereas in fact capitalism at the turn of the century appeared to have overcome its earlier tendency to crises.

---

1. Marx, *The German Ideology* (1845-1846) (New York: International, 1966), p. 49.

2. Major works include the English reformist J. A. Hobson, *Imperialism, a Study* (1902); and the Marxists, Rudolf Hilferding, *Finance Capital* (1910); Rosa Luxemburg, *The Accumulation of Capital* (1913); and V. I. Lenin, *Imperialism, the Highest Stage of Capitalism* (1916).

The theory of imperialism provided a Marxist solution to these difficulties. The effects predicted by classical Marxism derived from Marx's analysis of capitalism based on the assumption, already mentioned, of a closed system. But in imperialism, capitalism came into interaction with an external, precapitalist world. In finding new markets for its goods, new resources to develop, and new opportunities for capital investment, capitalism found ways to escape the effects predicted by classical Marxism. The imperialist extension of capitalism to Asia and Africa in a sense allowed capitalism to repeat its own youthful development on a grander scale. The persistence of middle classes, high wages, and high profits and also the avoidance of crises were to be expected in a time of capitalist growth, even on the models of classical Marxism.[3] In this way the theory of imperialism functioned to reconcile Marxist theory with observed reality. Imperialism functioned as a safety valve for capitalism.

The analysis of imperialism also had strategic implications for international socialism. Marxists had usually thought in terms of the socialist revolution as breaking out initially in the centers of advanced capitalism. This expectation was based on the thought that it would be there that the "contradictions" of capitalism would be most intense and that it would be there that the class consciousness of the proletariat would be most advanced. But the theory of imperialism suggested a different outlook. By allowing capitalism to expand, imperialism prevented the contradictions of capitalism from being felt in the capitalist centers. In particular, the high wages that growth produced discouraged the formation of revolutionary class consciousness among workers within the advanced capitalist countries. At the same time, imperial capitalism wreaked havoc on the precapitalist economies with which it came into contact. Traditional handicraft modes of production could not compete with lower-priced commodities flowing from the centers of industrial capitalism. And the displacement of land from the production of foodstuffs for local consumption to production of commodities for external markets (coffee, tea, cotton, bananas, and so forth) disrupted the supply of necessary goods for indigenous peoples. The results of the introduction of capitalism--separation of the people from the means of production, unemployment, and starvation--were the same as they had

---

3. Marx and Engels's own analysis of British imperialism in India point in this direction. Karl Marx and Frederick Engels, *On Colonialism* (New York: International, 1972). See also Marx's discussion, "The Modern Theory of Colonization," in *Capital* (1867), vol. 1 (New York: International, 1973), pp. 765-774.

been in Britain and Ireland a century earlier. Such desperate conditions might provoke a revolutionary response. The analysis of imperialism suggested that the international socialist revolution might work from the periphery inward rather than from the center outward.

Lenin's thought pushed Marxism further in this direction. In *Imperialism, the Highest Stage of Capitalism* (1916), Lenin applied the analysis of imperialism to questions of the war and the Social Democratic response to the war. Lenin's principal aims were to explain the war as the outcome of competition between capitalist states over division of the spoils of imperial domination and to connect the betrayal of socialist principles by the leaders of the Second International with the theme of a working class co-opted by imperialist capitalism. But Lenin also suggested the idea of conflict between the developed and the undeveloped parts of the world in which nation states stand in relationships of exploiter and exploited. "It is precisely the parasitism and decay of capitalism, characteristic of its highest stage of development, i.e., imperialism. As this pamphlet shows, capitalism has now singled out a *handful* (less than one-tenth of the inhabitants of the globe; less than one-fifth at a most generous and liberal calculation) of exceptionally rich and powerful states which plunder the whole world simply by 'clipping coupons.'"[4] Such a framework allows for an understanding of struggles for national liberation from the domination of the colonial powers as simultaneously class struggles against exploitation.

In 1919 the Bolsheviks had organized the Third International (the Comintern) as a "communist" alternative to the "socialist" Second International. At the Second Congress of the Third International in Moscow in 1920, Lenin suggested even more radical departures from the then-prevailing Marxism. Marxists had always conceived of the industrial proletariat as the class that would be the agent of socialist revolution. But in the colonized areas of the world this class, if it existed at all, was still a quite small proportion of the population as a whole. As in Russia the peasantry was by far the largest class throughout the colonized world. We have already seen how Lenin's openness to the potential revolutionary role of the peasants had led him to the idea of the October revolution in Russia, which with the support of workers and poor peasants would pass beyond the bourgeois revolution of February

---

4. V. I. Lenin, *Imperialism, the Highest Stage of Capitalism* (1916-1917) (Moscow: Progress, 1975), p. 13.

1917. In 1920 Lenin went further in suggesting Communist support for wholly peasant-based movements as a possible strategy for revolution.[5]

These ideas percolated through the discussions of the Third International during the early 1920s. At the Soviet-sponsored Baku Congress of Toilers of the East in 1920, for example, representatives of the Third International tried to find common ground with antiimperialists more at home with Islamic fundamentalism than with revolutionary Marxism. And Mir Syit Sultan-Galiyev, who became a Bolshevik soon after the October revolution, argued for an Islamic-based antiimperialist movement that would resist not only Western colonialism but also Soviet control in Central Asia.[6] This call for an independent antiimperialist movement was rejected by the leadership of the Third International, which continued to think in terms of a revolutionary movement of the toiling masses under the leadership of the proletariat and the international communist movement provided by the Communist Party of the Soviet Union.

In China these ideological and strategic controversies gained world-shaking practical significance. Plundered by the Western colonial powers, China had a history of antiimperialist struggle that reached back to the nineteenth century. Sun Yat-sen's Kuomintang, a political party rooted in the Revolutionary League organized in 1905, aimed at the liberation of China from foreign domination and the establishment of a democratic republic. Although Sun was himself influenced by Marx, it was not until 1921, inspired by the Bolshevik revolution in "backward" Russia, that a Marxist party was formed in China. In accord with the then-current thinking of the Third International, the Chinese Communist Party tried to form a base within the emerging Chinese working class and cooperated with the Kuomintang in its efforts to overcome foreign domination and establish a democratic republic.

During Sun's lifetime the Chinese Communists were able to gain a strong position within the Kuomintang. But after Sun's death in 1925 and the ascension to leadership of Chiang Kai-shek, relationships between Communists and non-Communists within the Kuomintang became strained by competition for power. In 1927 Chiang ordered a massacre of Chinese Communists. In spite of this the leadership of the Third International continued to recommend that the Chinese

---

5.   Adam Westoby, *The Evolution of Communism* (New York: Free Press, 1989), p. 69.

6.   On the Baku Congress, see Westoby, *Evolution of Communism*, p. 69. On Sultan-Galiyev see Leszek Kolakowski, *Main Currents of Marxism* (Oxford: Clarendon Press, 1978), vol. 3, p. 19.

Communists cooperate with the Kuomintang, and for some time efforts were made to reach an understanding with forces within the Kuomintang that were less hostile to the Communists. But eventually, in accordance with the turn in thinking adopted at the Sixth Congress of the Third International in 1928, the Chinese Communists abandoned cooperation with the Kuomintang in favor of a policy of independent action for the cause of revolutionary communism.

The change of direction adopted by the Third International in 1928 was connected with the change of direction within the Soviet Union. By the time of Lenin's death, it was apparent that the tide of revolution had crested. This development meant that, contrary to everyone's expectations, the building of socialism would have to proceed in a single, politically isolated, and economically backward country. It also meant that Communist parties outside the Soviet Union would have to operate under nonrevolutionary conditions. From the time of Lenin's death until 1928, when Stalin again called for requisition of grain from the peasants, the Communist Party of the Soviet Union followed an internal policy of cooperation with non-Communist elements. This was the period of the New Economic Policy and of relative freedom for non-Communist cultural currents. This same "cooperative" mode governed the direction of the Communist Third International during this period of time. So, for example, in China, as we have seen, the Third International encouraged Chinese Communists to cooperate with non-Communist elements within the Kuomintang. Beginning in 1928, fearing that the "socialist" direction of Soviet development was threatened by a class of independent farmers growing in economic power, the Communist Party of the Soviet Union had changed from a policy of cooperation with non-Communist elements to a policy aimed at complete Communist control. The change in direction within the international movement was motivated by similar considerations. Thinking that the capitalist world faced an imminent economic, and consequently also political, crisis, the leadership of the Third International came to the conclusion that revolutionary possibilities were once again on the horizon. And applying the lessons of the Bolshevik revolution, they also came to the conclusion that, in such a climate, it was important for Communist parties around the world to sharply distinguish their own revolutionary program from the hesitant and muddled reformism of other parties that appealed to the working class. Accordingly, following the Sixth Congress of the Communist International, Communist parties around the world changed from a policy of cooperation with reformists to a policy of competition for the support of the working class and for independent political action.

In China this took the form of the Communist Party's finally abandoning attempts to cooperate with the Kuomintang and attempting to form its own independent base by organizing the small Chinese working class. However, one of the founders of the Chinese Communist Party followed a strategy independent from this thinking of the Third International. As early as January 1927--before the break with the Kuomintang, before the change of direction of the Third International, and contrary to the working-class base recommended by communist theory--Mao Tse-tung extolled the potential for Chinese communism of a peasant-based revolutionary movement.[7]

Under the political leadership of Mao, some Chinese Communists began the task of organizing this revolutionary peasant movement. There were essentially two tasks. One was to gain political support from the masses of poor peasants. The other was to form an army capable of fighting for power. These two tasks were interconnected. The political work of the Communist cadre involved organizing within peasant villages. Communists spoke in favor of land reform that would take land from the rich and powerful peasants and give land to the poor and formerly powerless peasants. Communists also spoke against feudal relationships of subordination: between poor peasants and their landlords, between peasants and local powerful men (whether representatives or the government of local "warlords"), between women and men, and between children and parents. The Communists urged the poor and downtrodden to speak out against those who oppressed and exploited them. They encouraged the formation of cooperatives. And they recruited leaders of the poor peasants into active roles in the formation of cooperatives, the re-distribution of land, and the formation of local political institutions independent of external forces. Such changes involved a radical upheaval of village life. They challenged the rich and powerful elites that had governed village life in the past. Poor peasants could be expected to become involved in such things only if there was some prospect that these changes could be defended against the forces that would inevitably be arrayed against them. Thus it was necessary that an armed force be organized to protect the changes made. But it was also true that the political program served as a powerful base for recruitment for the military force. Seeing what changes the Communists brought, poor peasants were willing to join the Communist armed forces. Gradually the revolution spread throughout the Chinese

---

7.   Mao Tse-tung, "Report on an Investigation of the Peasant Movement in Hunan," in *Selected Works of Mao Tse-Tung*, vol. 1 (Peking: Foreign Languages Press, 1965), pp. 23-59.

countryside. Except for a period of cooperation in struggle against the Japanese during World War II, the Kuomintang and the Communists fought against one another for control of China for some twenty years. In the end, having the support of the rural masses, the Chinese Communists won in 1949.[8]

The Chinese revolution provided a model that, suitably adjusted to the demands of local history and circumstances, strongly influenced similar revolutionary movements in other countries. In Indonesia and Vietnam, for example, strong Communist movements were developed that shared with the Chinese example their Communist leadership, peasant base, and antiimperialist orientation. Such movements were very different from the urban industrial working-class revolutions envisaged by Marx and Engels. But they were not completely foreign to classical Marxism. They shared with classical Marxism a belief that political systems, and the cultural ideology that legitimated them, reflected the struggle of classes rooted in the economic system of production. And they shared with classical Marxism an ideal vision of a cooperative society in which a highly developed system of productive forces would be collectively managed for the good of all by means of a democratically planned economy. In the analysis of imperialism Communist leaders found the theoretical means of reconciling their own political movements with the classical Marxist theory of capitalism.

The Bolshevik revolution provided a pivotal link between classical Marxism and the kind of agrarian Communist movements modeled on the Chinese revolution. This is true in a number of respects. First, classical Marxism was ambivalent about imperialism. On the one hand, Marx clearly regarded imperialist exploitation with disgust and moral outrage. But on the other, he sometimes suggested that the evils of imperialism were historically necessary and that consequently it was a mistake to try to oppose Western imperialism. As we have seen, this ambivalent heritage led to conflicting views within the Second International, with some Marxists, such as Bernstein, defending European colonialism, and others, such as Lenin, denouncing it. Second, the Bolshevik revolution was itself a mixed revolution, including both antifeudal and antiimperialist currents as well as anticapitalist currents. In this respect, and in the subsequent rapid development of its economic,

---

8.   Edgar Snow, *Red Star Over China* (New York: Bantam, 1978), provides an account of the rise to power of Chinese Communism. William Hinton, *Fanshen* (New York: Vintage, 1966), provides a rich account of the process of revolutionary change in a single Chinese village.

scientific, and technical capabilities, the Soviet experience provided a model for Third World countries bent on achieving both rapid development and freedom from imperial control. Third, with the Leninist theory of the party, Third World revolutionary movements found the organizational means to lead a revolutionary movement under economically and politically "backward" conditions. It is thus not surprising that Marxism in the Third World followed a Leninist rather than a non-Leninist course. While many Western socialists acquiesced in or even supported Western colonialism, Leninists resolutely opposed it. While Socialists clung to the supposed necessary sequence of stages-- feudalism, capitalism, socialism--Communists raised the possibility of an immediate alternative to capitalist exploitation. And while Socialists appeared everywhere to be ineffectual parliamentary minorities, Communists had proven their ability to successfully gain real power. Or at least, so it appeared to many Third World revolutionaries.

The years following World War II brought with them not only the success of peasant-based communist movements in China, Korea, and Vietnam but also the formation of Communist states in Eastern Europe. Although in some countries, such as Yugoslavia and Albania, Communist regimes grew out of indigenous forces, elsewhere the Communist regimes in Eastern Europe were imposed by Soviet military force. In some countries, such as Czechoslovakia and Germany, Communist regimes were able to build on existing Communist parties with some support in a developed industrial working class.[9] In other countries there was no industrial working class of significant size. In Poland the Communist Party had been almost completely destroyed.[10]

Throughout Eastern Europe the new regimes were led by minority Communist parties built on the remnants of prewar Communist parties and an influx of new members in the postwar period. Some of these new members were attracted to the Communist Party on idealistic grounds. Many others joined as a way of furthering their careers. In Hungary

---

9. In Czechoslovakia, for example, in the free elections in 1946 the Communists won 38 percent of the vote. See Daniel Singer, "Czechoslovakia's Quiet Revolution," *Nation* 250:4 (January 29, 1990), p. 122.

10. The destruction of the Communist Party of Poland was one of the outcomes of the nonaggression pact signed between Germany and the Soviet Union in August 1939. Polish Communists fleeing the Nazi invasion of Poland were either imprisoned or executed by Soviet authorities or turned over to German authorities where a similar fate awaited them. On this matter, see Romuald Spasowski, *The Liberation of One* (San Diego: Harcourt Brace Jovanovich, 1986), pp. 115-154, for the experiences of one Polish Communist during this time.

membership in the Communist Party increased from "barely a dozen" in 1942 to 500,000 by the end of 1945.[11] In Czechoslovakia in 1946 sixteen-year-old Zdeněk Mlynář joined the Communist Party convinced that the world was torn by a struggle between good and evil in which Stalin led the forces of good.[12] And in Poland young Romuald Spasowski, the son of an idealistic communist philosopher, formed a local Communist Party Committee, convinced that "outside the Party there would be little opportunity to influence events."[13]

The Communist regimes of Eastern Europe, modeled on the Soviet system, were not democratic. As events developed, idealists like Mlynář and Spasowski struggled to transform communism in Eastern Europe. Defeated, they abandoned the Communist Party. The career-minded opportunists hung on, doing whatever was necessary to maintain positions in parties that were ultimately dependent on the threat of Soviet intervention for their political power. For some forty years the Communist regimes of Eastern Europe served as specters of unfreedom. Their existence provided a pretext for a policy of containment of communism by the United States and Western Europe. This struggle against communism would significantly color American life in the decades following World War II.

---

11. Westoby, *The Evolution of Communism*, pp. 111-112. Westoby points out that some of those who joined the Hungarian Communist Party at this time were opportunistic converts from fascism who saw in the Hungarian Communist Party opportunities for personal advancement. But Westoby does not claim that this accounts for all or even most of the gains made by the Communists. He mentions the experience of the war and economic ruin as contributing to support for the Communists.

12. Zdeněk Mlynář, *Nightfrost in Prague* (New York: Karz, 1980), pp. 1-2.

13. Romuald Spasowski, *Liberation of One*, p. 229.

8

Communism and Anticommunism in the United States

The year 1912 was in several ways a turning point in the history of American socialism. Socialist electoral victories reflected the swelling tide of reformism in U.S. politics. But Socialist successes in cities across the country alarmed leaders of the established parties and led them to unite against Socialists. Fear of Socialists, and especially fear of their immigrant "foreign" supporters, fueled support for "reforms" of local government aimed at replacing partisan ward-based systems of representation with "commission" forms of government in which elections were nonpartisan and city wide. By diluting Socialist votes such reforms deprived Socialists of their offices based on support in working-class neighborhoods. And Socialists in power were themselves subject to unanticipated conflicting forces. Did they represent the working class or the citizenry as a whole? Were they bound by party discipline to adhere to positions adopted by local Socialists? Attempts to respond to these questions were bound to alienate some voters, either Socialists or non-Socialist allies who did not fully accept Socialist positions.[1]

In the years between 1912 and World War I the tensions between "native" and immigrant socialism returned to haunt American socialism. Waves of immigration in the late nineteenth and early twentieth centuries had produced a working class that was largely made up of immigrants or sons and daughters of immigrants. Many of these immigrant workers--among them Slavs, Italians, Poles, Finns, and Jews-- were not accepted by "native" Americans. Viewed with a mixture of fear and disgust grounded in ignorance and racism, many of these workers

---

1. See Richard W. Judd, *Socialist Cities* (Albany: State University of New York Press, 1989), pp. 41, 106, 138.

found themselves herded into inferior living conditions and excluded from American institutions. Such workers often saw the Socialist Party as their champion, and in large numbers they joined the party. But steeped in the "native" American cultural milieu, American socialism was itself contaminated with the antiforeign attitudes of the surrounding society. This is not to say that all Socialists shared these prejudices. But many did. And even those who did not failed to give sufficient weight to the distinct cultural values and needs of immigrant Americans. It was not until 1912 that the Socialist Party of America admitted foreign-language Socialist federations as autonomous units.[2]

After 1912 immigrant workers, organized into these foreign-language Socialist federations, became an increasingly large proportion of Socialist Party membership. By the time of the United States' entry into World War I, "foreigners" constituted approximately half of the membership of the party.

U.S. entry into World War I brought great difficulties to American Socialists. We have already seen how most of the European socialist parties abandoned their principles and patriotically supported the war effort of their respective countries. On April 8, 1917, one day after the U.S. Congress declared war against Germany, American Socialists, meeting in convention in St. Louis, voted overwhelmingly to oppose the war and to expel any Socialist representatives who voted in favor of funding the U.S. war effort. The convention made the Socialist position clear: "We brand the declaration of war by our government as a crime against the people of the United States and against the nations of the world."[3]

Because of its largely "foreign" membership, and because of the European (and especially German) roots of the socialist movement, the Socialist Party was attacked as a traitor to the American nation by the government, the press, and the American Federation of Labor. Many English-language intellectuals, who had supported the party in the past, now abandoned it. Socialist newspapers were banned from the mail under the espionage act of 1917. Mobs of patriotic citizens attacked Socialist speakers and Socialist offices. Much of the national leadership was arrested and many Socialists were sent to prison. For his courageous speech against the war in Canton, Ohio, in June 1918, Eugene

---

2.   Judd, *Socialist Cities*, pp. 31-32, 79-83; Paul Buhle, *Marxism in the United States* (London: Verso, 1991), pp. 112-113.
3.   Albert Fried, *Socialism in America* (Garden City: Anchor, 1970), p. 507.

Debs, the great standard-bearer for the Socialists in presidential elections, was sentenced to ten years in prison.

An even more-violent repression fell on the Industrial Workers of the World, which had taken a similarly militant position in opposition to the war. Bill Haywood and other leaders of the IWW were sentenced to twenty year prison terms. IWW organizer Frank Little was lynched. In Centralia, Washington, armed American Legionnaires attacked an IWW hall. Everywhere across the United States, government, press, and patriotic mobs attacked the IWW, the Wobblies.

The wave of repression against the Socialists and the IWW culminated in the Palmer raids of 1919 and 1920. In a series of coordinated nighttime raids in cities across the United States, 10,000 Socialists, Wobblies, and innocent "foreigners" were seized, often violently abused, and detained by officers under the direction of the attorney general of the United States. This internal repression, accompanied as it was with the sending of U.S. armed forces to intervene on the side of the "whites" in the Russian civil war, was the opening salvo in a war on communism which would largely guide American policy for the next seventy years.

Like its European counterparts, the American Communist Party was born in this era of World War I and the Bolshevik revolution. As in Europe in 1919 the American Socialist Party split into two camps: the Socialists, who rejected the Leninist model for party organization, and the Communists, who followed the Leninist model. In fact, there were originally two Communist parties in the United States, made up of rival contenders for the mantle of revolutionary communism. In each of these, the Communist Party and the Communist Labor Party, elements from the foreign-language federations of the presplit Socialist Party played significant roles. Large numbers of Jews, Russians, Slavs, Finns, and Scandinavians entered the communist movement in the United States. Locked in lower-level jobs, discriminated against by the native English-speaking culture, and excluded from positions of power by legal and cultural barriers, immigrant Americans found in communism a system of ideas that explained the world of their experience and an "internationalist" openness to their own cross-cultural identities.

The development of the communist movement in the United States was strongly influenced by the policies of the Communist Third International, just as was the communist movement in other parts of the world. United by the direction of the International during the early 1920s, in the middle 1920s the American Communist Party followed the policy of cooperation with reform currents in the American labor movement and the American political parties, although these efforts were hampered by factionalism and heavy-handedness within the Party and by anticommunism outside it.

In line with the international change of direction initiated by the Soviets at the Sixth Congress of the International in 1928, the American Communist Party at this time jettisoned its former leadership and the policies of cooperation with reformers that it had been following. For the next five years the party followed the internationally prescribed course of independent action aimed at sharply distinguishing Communists from reformers and at preparing for an impending revolutionary struggle. During these years the American Communists denounced all other American political parties, including such radical parties as the Farmer-Labor Party and the Socialist Party.

In 1935, at its Seventh Congress, the Communist International took another sharp turn in its policies. Again, as with the turn adopted in 1928, there was a domestic Soviet dimension to this change in international policy. From 1928 through 1934, as we have seen, internal Soviet policy aimed at collectivization of agriculture and at "cleansing" Soviet life and culture by replacing nonpolitical specialists with committed revolutionaries. This was a time of struggle and confrontation between the Communist Party and cultural groups or individuals outside the control of the Party. Beginning in 1934, there was a certain relaxation of tension in the confrontational policies of the Party. In the same way, in the international sphere, 1935 marked a change from confrontation to renewed attempts at cooperation with political forces outside the Party. This was the beginning of the period of the "popular front" policy in the international Communist movement.

One aspect of the popular front was the attempt to form an alliance of "democratic" or "progressive" groups against the rising tide of European fascism. By 1935, with the Nazis firmly in control and with Communist leadership imprisoned, the popular front policy was largely irrelevant in Germany and Italy. But in other countries, the new policy played a significant role. By putting an end to Communist attacks on socialists and reformers of various kinds, the popular front policy opened the door for Communists to work with non-Communists in government, trade unions, and a broad array of cultural organizations.

In France, for example, the popular front policy adopted by the Communists in 1935 paid political dividends as early as the election of 1936. In a historic breakthrough the Popular Front coalition won the national election, with the Socialists winning 149 seats in parliament and the Communists and the (in U.S. terms, "liberal") Radicals, their coalition allies, winning 72 and 109 seats respectively. On the basis of these election results the Socialist Leon Blum headed a coalition government that was able to respond to the economic crisis of the depression with a series of measures aimed at improving the position of the working class. Of fundamental and lasting importance, for example, was government enforcement of the right of workers to collective bargaining. Other steps included 12 percent wage increases, a forty-hour work week, two-week vacations with pay, and public works for the unemployed. Such measures brought desperately needed relief for French workers but also served to isolate fascist and extreme right-wing groups in French political life. Most working people stood solidly behind a reformist government committed to democracy and the protection of fundamental human rights. In Germany the Communists had been crushed as an isolated fringe of the national political life. In France, where the popular front policy had a chance, Communists played a significant role in shaping the national response to the crises of economic depression and fascist politics.

In Spain in the elections of 1936 popular front policies led to the formation of a democratic coalition government. As in France, the popular front coalition in Spain aimed both at improving the lot of the working people of Spain and at rallying all democratic forces against right-wing attacks. But in Spain the right wing was more broadly and more deeply entrenched in the fabric of national life. A military revolt against the republican government--a revolt led by Francisco Franco that drew on the support of monarchists, fascists, the army, and the church--dragged Spain into a long and terrible civil war. In spite of a war of defense by the Spanish republicans in which the Communists played a significant role, in spite of the aid of international brigades largely organized by Communists, and in spite of aid from the Soviet Union, the Francoists, heavily supported by the fascist governments of Germany and Italy, eventually triumphed.

A contributing cause to the downfall of the Spanish Republic was the embargo on arms shipments to the republic adopted by the United States and other democratic countries. The aim of this embargo was to force an end to the Spanish civil war. But with Germany and Italy aiding the Spanish fascists, the effect of the embargo was to aid the antirepublican side in the civil war. In the Congress of the United States, the sole vote against the embargo on arms for the Spanish Republic was cast by a young congressman from the eighth district of Minnesota. Elected in 1936 with the support of Communists, acting in accord with the popular front policy in support of the Farmer-Labor Party in Minnesota, John T. Bernard in a sense represented the historical forces and possibilities released by depression-era popular front politics.

The son of immigrant Corsican parents, John Bernard grew up on the Iron Range of Minnesota, an area with deep roots in the immigrant radicalism of the IWW, the American Socialist Party, and the American Communist Party. Beaten down in the strikes of 1907 and 1916, harassed by imprisonments and deportations during World War I and the Palmer raids, Iron Range radicals had begun to gain control of local governments during the 1920s under the banner of the Farmer-Labor Party of Minnesota. During the period from 1928 to 1935 the radical forces were split by Communist opposition to the Farmer-Labor Party. But with the change of direction adopted by the Communists in 1935, the way was open for a united-left response to the depression, which was radicalizing growing numbers of Minnesotans. It was this unity in response to radicalizing conditions that led to the election of Bernard in 1936.

Because of his background in the Iron Range politics of a radically conscious and multinational working class, Bernard was able to think and act in terms that went beyond the usual intellectual and geographical localism of members of Congress. His vote against the embargo on arms for the Spanish Republic is one sign of this. Another was his support for sit-in strikers at General Motors in Flint, Michigan, in early 1937. Although many U.S. politicians viewed the sit-down strike as a violation of private property and virtually all of them denounced the violence accompanying the strike, Congressman Bernard went to Flint, climbed through a window, and joined the strikers on the plant floor.[4]

The U.S. auto industry, like most basic U.S. industries at the time, was nonunion. Its working force was made up largely of immigrants, sons of immigrants, blacks, and other unskilled laborers. Such workers fell outside the bounds of the craft unions in the American Federation of Labor. Efforts to form industrial unions that would include these workers had appeared repeatedly on the American scene, from the National Labor Union and the Knights of Labor to the American Railway Union of Eugene V. Debs and the industrial unionism of the IWW. From the time of its beginning in the 1919 split of the American Socialist Party, industrial unionism had also been central to the American Communist Party. Although the party had some success in organizing unions in industries with a radical immigrant work force, like the fur industry, until the popular front period, Communists remained a fringe element in the U.S. labor movement. Following the change to the popular front

---

4.   On John Bernard, see "A Common Man's Courage," a biographical video by John De Graff available in the library of the University of Minnesota, Duluth.

policy in 1935, Communists were ready to join in the drive to organize basic U.S. industries launched by the Congress for Industrial Organization (CIO) in the fall of that year.

The depression that struck the U.S. economy in late 1929 brought massive unemployment and declining wages in the early 1930s. The depression exposed the relative backwardness of U.S. institutions. The safety nets of extended families, fraternal benevolent societies, and religious charities that had protected workers throughout the 1920s were overwhelmed by the demands placed on them by the depression. Lacking any federal relief programs, municipal and county governments were faced with demands they, too, were unable to meet.[5]

At the time the depression struck the U.S. economy, most American workers were unorganized. Attempts by radicals to organize the masses of industrial workers had foundered on the strong antiunionism of American big business and the indifference of the American Federation of Labor, which saw in industrial unions only a threat to its own principles of craft unionism. In addition to denouncing radical attempts at forming industrial unions as betrayals of the American labor movement, the AFL stoutly resisted reformist proposals for government interference and regulation of labor markets. As late as 1932, for example, the AFL opposed government programs for unemployment compensation. It is not surprising, then, that the first depression-era attempts to organize industrial workers came from outside the AFL.

The National Industrial Recovery Act of 1933 had included federal recognition of the right of workers to organize unions for the purpose of collective bargaining. This step provided a clear legal foundation for union organizing in basic industries that had so far refused to bargain collectively with independent worker-controlled labor unions. But this step alone was not sufficient to win unionization of U.S. industries. A difficult struggle remained.

That struggle commenced in May 1934. In Toledo, Ohio, striking Auto-Lite workers defied a court injunction against union picketing that would have allowed strike-breaking scab workers to enter the plant. The National Guard was called in to enforce the injunction. When workers resisted, a six-day battle resulted in which two workers were killed and many injured. But in the end, the strikers won both a contract and company recognition of their union as a legitimate representative for

---

5. For a discussion of these supportive institutions and the effects of their breakdown in Chicago, see Lizabeth Cohen, *Making A New Deal: Industrial Workers in Chicago, 1919-1939* (Cambridge: Cambridge University Press, 1990).

purposes of collective bargaining. In this case, the union formed did join the American Federation of Labor. But the leadership for the strike had come from outside the AFL. Specifically, key leadership came from A. J. Muste, a clergyman, labor educator, and independent socialist, at that time working with American Trotskyists who had left or been expelled from the American Communist Party.[6]

Also in May 1934 an important strike broke out among the teamsters of Minneapolis and St. Paul, Minnesota. Organized along industrial lines, including not only drivers of trucks but also dock, warehouse, and other workers, the strike was opposed by the leaders of the AFL International Brotherhood of Teamsters. Leadership for the strike in Teamsters Local 574 was provided by three brothers--Vincent, Grant, and Miles Dunne--and by Carl Skogland, all of whom were Trotskyists. Opposed by the proemployer Citizens Alliance, the strike had the overwhelming support of workers and their families. For nearly three months the strikers fought a shifting battle with forces from the Citizens Alliance and the police, a battle in which two strikers were killed and many more injured. In the end, the strikers won.[7]

May 1934 also saw the beginning of a major strike among the longshoremen of San Francisco. Again, the strike was led by radicals outside the AFL. This time leadership was provided by Harry Bridges who had ties to the American Communist Party. Again, in spite of the opposition of William Green, the national president of the AFL, the strike had overwhelming support among West Coast longshoremen. After a violent confrontation with police that resulted in the death of two strikers, San Francisco workers virtually shut down the city with a two-day general strike. In late July the strike ended with an arbitrated settlement that was followed by union victories all along the West Coast the following year.[8]

In late 1935, responding to the mood of militancy at the grass roots, trade unionists within the AFL sympathetic to the cause of industrial unionism formed the Congress for Industrial Organization. Led by John L. Lewis of the United Mine Workers (UMW) and including Philip

---

6. For an account of this strike by Art Preis, a Trotskyist activist and leader of the strike, see Art Preis, *Labor's Giant Step* (New York: Pathfinder Press, 1972), pp. 17-24.

7. Ibid., pp. 24-30, provides an account of the Twin Cities truckers' strike. See also Farrell Dobbs, *Teamster Rebellion* (New York: Monad Press, 1972). Dobbs was one of the leaders of the strike.

8. Ibid., pp. 31-33. Another account of this strike is provided by Richard Boyer and Herbert Morais, *Labor's Untold Story* (New York: United Electrical Radio and Machine Workers of America, 1979), pp. 282-289.

Murray of the UMW, David Dubinsky of the International Ladies Garment Workers, and Sidney Hillman of the Amalgamated Clothing Workers, the CIO aimed at the organization of the masses of unorganized workers in basic American industries. Targeting the steel industry for its initial effort, the CIO sent over 400 organizers into the field, opened thirty-five regional offices, and began publication of *Steel Labor*, a newspaper designed to promote the organizing drive.

But as it turned out, grass-roots pressure for unionization made the automotive industry, not steel, the initial test for the CIO. First established in 1935 with a leadership appointed by William Green of the AFL, the United Auto Workers (UAW) sharply changed its direction at its convention in 1936. Overriding President Francis Dillon, the convention voted to seat left-wing delegates from Toledo and elected Homer Martin to replace Dillon as president of the union. Two key UAW organizers, Robert Travis and Wyndham Mortimer, were close to the American Communist Party. In working with them and in expressly defeating a resolution to bar Communists from the union, the UAW openly welcomed Communist Party, Trotskyist, and other radical activists into the new union. These radicals were to play key roles in sustaining the difficult struggle to organize the auto workers. During winter 1936-1937, auto workers in General Motors (GM) plants engaged in a series of sit-down strikes in which striking workers occupied the plants and striking pickets outside the plants supported the workers inside. It was such a strike that Congressman Bernard climbed through a window to join. In February 1937, following a series of tense and sometimes violent confrontations around key GM plants in Flint, Michigan, the UAW won union recognition and a union contract.[9]

Over the course of the next few years the CIO organizing drive brought unions to some 6 million previously unorganized U.S. workers. Steelworkers, iron miners, packinghouse workers, electrical workers, lumberjacks, woodworkers, furniture makers, rubber workers, utility workers, paper workers, and others marched under the banner of the CIO. In many cases, unions were achieved only after difficult and often violent strikes. On Memorial Day, 1937, for example, police fired into crowds of unarmed men, women, and children parading in support of the effort to organize Republic Steel plants on the south side of Chicago,

---

9. Preis, *Labor's Giant Step*, pp. 50-61; Boyer and Morais, *Labor's Untold Story*, pp. 298-309. On the role of the Communists in the UAW, see Roger Keeran, *The Communist Party and the Auto Workers' Union* (New York: International, 1980).

killing ten and wounding thirty others.[10] The great victories achieved by the CIO were won because millions of American workers and their families were willing to take their places on the picket lines and in the meeting halls. Although depression conditions created a sense of emergency and of the need for radical action, the personal commitment to struggle and to the risks that were involved necessarily drew on each individual's sense of justice and solidarity with other workers.

Also instrumental in the victories of the CIO were the efforts of hundreds of radical organizers who took upon themselves the additional burdens and risks of leadership. As we have seen, Communists, Trotskyists, and other radicals played key roles in the Auto-Lite, truckers, and longshoremen's strikes of 1934 and in the initial CIO fight to organize the auto workers. Radicals played key leadership roles in most of the other struggles as well. Although the top leadership of the CIO was not Communist, Communists and other radicals provided much of the grass-roots leadership and much of the regional and intermediate leadership as well. The extent of Communist Party influence on the CIO is indicated by the claim, no doubt somewhat exaggerated, of Communist Party Chairman Earl Browder that "the Communists had the initiative on all important questions in the CIO."[11]

In the period of the popular front, American Communists played a significant role in the trade union movement, in the political parties of some states, in a variety of ethnic organizations, in a myriad of antifascist groups, and in American cultural life. The period was the heyday of American Communism.[12] During this period Party Chairman Browder and individual Communist activists struggled to convince the American people that Communists were part of the American mainstream backing President Franklin D. Roosevelt, both in his New Deal reforms and in his opposition to European fascism.

In August 1939, the Soviet Union signed a nonaggression pact with Nazi Germany. Following Moscow's lead, Communists around the world abruptly abandoned their antifascist agitation. In the United

---

10. Boyer and Morais, *Labor's Untold Story*, pp. 314-315.
11. Quoted in Philip Jaffe, *The Rise and Fall of American Communism* (New York: Horizon Press, 1975), p. 143. On the important role of Communist organizers in the Chicago area CIO, see Cohen, *Making a New Deal*, pp. 308-313. Harvey Klehr and John Haynes, in *The American Communist Movement* (New York: Twayne, 1992), pp. 82-83, tell us that more than a quarter of the organizers involved in the CIO campaign to organize the steel industry were Communists and that about 40 percent of all CIO unions had significant Communist connections.
12. Harvey Klehr, *The Heyday of American Communism* (New York: Basic Books, 1984).

States, Communists threw their support to those who opposed U.S. entry into the war against the fascist powers. In 1941, Germany broke the nonaggression pact and invaded the Soviet Union. Again following Moscow's lead, American Communists made another abrupt turn, returning to the antifascist cause and urging the Roosevelt administration to take a more active role in the war.

With the decision by the Browder-led American Communist Party to dissolve itself following U.S. entry into World War II, the popular front strategy reached its extreme expression. Convinced that furthering the military alliance between the Soviet Union and the Western democracies against fascism was the paramount duty of all progressive people, the American Communist Party did everything it could to support the U.S. war effort. Dissolution of the party as a political alternative to the Democratic Party of President Franklin D. Roosevelt was part of this effort. A pledge of no strikes for the duration of the war was another part of it. Browder himself sought to continue the cooperative relationship between the Communists and the U.S. government into the postwar years. But this was not to be. The abrupt turns in American Communist policies in the years just prior to the war had made clear that the American Communist Party's principal loyalty was to the Soviet-led international Communist movement. As the wartime collaboration between the United States and the Soviet Union gave way to cold war confrontation, the American Communists found themselves isolated and treated as enemies of America.

As the major powers to emerge from the war, the United States and the Soviet Union stood as champions for two rival systems and as contending centers of power. By 1950 regimes modeled on the Soviet system had been established throughout Eastern Europe, the Communists had won against the U.S.-backed forces of Chiang Kai-shek in China, U.S. soldiers were fighting communism in Korea, and the United States and the Soviet Union were locked in a tense contest of will and resources that came to be known as the cold war. In the United States the American Communist Party, following the lead of Moscow, deposed Browder, who had urged continued collaboration with American capitalism, and under the leadership of William Z. Foster, prepared to do battle as an ally of the Soviet Union in the struggle against capitalism and imperialism.[13]

Determined to contain any further advance of communism, the United States repeatedly used its military power to defeat supposed Communist

---

13. For an account of this period, see Jaffe, *Rise and Fall*, pp. 69-85.

or Communist-supported political movements around the world. In Iran in 1952 the United States supported a coup against the elected government of Muhammad Mussadegh that restored the military dictatorship of the shah.[14] In Guatemala in 1954, in the name of anticommunism, the United States supported a military coup that overthrew the elected government of Jacob Arbenz. In 1961 U.S.-backed forces invaded Cuba, hoping to overthrow the Communist government of Fidel Castro. In 1965 U.S. forces landed in the Dominican Republic to prevent the restoration of the elected reformer Juan Bosch, who had previously been overthrown by a military coup.[15]   Also in 1965 the United States gave its blessing to the military coup led by Suharto in Indonesia. The coup was followed by the murder of hundreds of thousands of suspected Indonesian Communists and their supporters. Throughout the 1960s and early 1970s U.S. military aid and military advisers assisted in the "anticommunist" suppression of left-wing opposition groups throughout much of Latin America. In 1973 U.S. support played a part in the bloody coup that overthrew the elected government of the Marxist Salvador Allende and instigated a violently repressive military dictatorship in Chile.[16] In Africa throughout the 1970s and 1980s the United States supported military opposition to Marxists in Angola and Mozambique. In 1983 U.S. forces invaded Grenada and overthrew its Marxist government. And throughout the 1980s U.S. aid maintained a military opposition force that bled the meager human and economic resources of the left-wing Sandinista regime in Nicaragua. By far the biggest of these military adventures aimed at containing communism was the U.S. war against Vietnam. Fought under the pretext of preventing the imposition of communism on the democracy of South Vietnam, the U.S. effort in fact flagrantly violated the letter and the spirit of the Geneva accords of 1954 that put an end to French colonialism in Vietnam.[17]

---

14.   On U.S. involvement in the coup in Iran, see Kermit Roosevelt, *Countercoup: The Struggle for the Control of Iran* (New York: McGraw-Hill, 1979).

15.   For accounts of American involvement in Guatemala and the Dominican Republic, see John Gerrasi, *The Great Fear in Latin America* (New York: Collier-Macmillan, 1968).

16.   Richard Helms, who was director of the U.S. Central Intelligence Agency at the time of the coup pleaded no contest to legal charges that he failed to testify fully about CIA activities in Chile during his 1973 testimony before the Senate Foreign Relations Committee.

17.   The Geneva accords of 1954 provided for the separation of Vietnamese and French forces by a military dividing line, but the Accords went on to say that "the military demarcation line is provisional and should not in any way be interpreted as constituting a political or territorial boundary." Point 6, Final Declaration, July 21, 1954. And the Accords

While U.S. foreign policy aimed at the containment of communism, internal American policy aimed at destroying the influence of Communists on American life. In 1947 the Taft-Hartley Act both reduced the power of the unions and, by requiring non-Communist oaths of all union officials, purged all Communists from positions of leadership in the unions. In the wild charges of Senator Joseph McCarthy and in the hearings before the House Un-American Activities Committee of the U.S. Congress, frightened radicals, paid informers, sensation-seeking individuals, vindictive liars, and baseless rumor-mongers contributed to the destruction of Communists and non-Communists alike. Public school teachers, university professors, actors, writers, and others were fired and blacklisted on account of their political beliefs.[18] The leadership of the Communist Party was sent to prison. And two Communists, Ethel and Julius Rosenberg, were executed for giving military secrets to the Soviets.

The collaborationist policy of the popular front had, in a sense, worked too well. Alarmed at the apparent successes of Communists at home and around the globe, American capitalism fought back. To be sure, Soviet Communism was fundamentally incompatible with America's democratic traditions. But the American response used the cause of anticommunism to justify the repression even of those movements, Communist and non-Communist, that could rightly claim widespread popular support. In the name of defending democracy U.S. foreign policy often served the cause of profoundly undemocratic elites. Meanwhile at home, in the name of liberty, the anti-Communist campaign committed serious violations of the liberties of U.S. citizens.

---

provided for elections to determine the government of the whole of Vietnam that were to follow in July of 1956. Point 7, Final Declaration. For the text of these points in the Geneva accords, see George Kahn and John Lewis, *The United States in Vietnam* (New York: Dell, 1969), p. 442. On the promised elections, see Kahn and Lewis, *United States in Vietnam*, pp. 80-87. It was the U.S.-backed regime of Ngo Diem that refused to participate in the election process. Even though recognizing that it was generally assumed at the time of the accords that the Communists under Ho Chi Minh would eventually govern all of Vietnam, George Carver, no friend of the Vietnamese Communists, justified U.S. and South Vietnamese refusal to permit elections on grounds that the Geneva accords did not specify what the election was to be about and on grounds that neither the U.S. nor the South Vietnamese government had signed the accords. George Carver, "The Faceless Viet Cong," *Foreign Affairs*, 44:3 (April 1966), pp. 355-356. Dwight Eisenhower, *Mandate for Change* (Garden City: Doubleday, 1963), p. 353, cites the uncertainty of Vietnamese support for such a move as a reason against U.S. military intervention in Vietnam.

18. David Caute, *The Great Fear: The Anti-Communist Purge Under Truman and Eisenhower* (New York: Simon and Schuster, 1978); Victor Navasky, *Naming Names* (New York: Viking, 1980); Lillian Hellman, *Scoundrel Time* (New York: Bantam, 1977).

For some forty years this cold war conflict between Western capitalism and Eastern communism dominated world affairs. On the surface, at least, the contending parties appeared to be locked in their positions. But beneath the surface, forces for change were at work in the communist world. Among these forces was an effort to reform the Soviet model and create a form of socialism more in keeping with the emancipatory aspirations of the socialist tradition. In the next chapter we will examine this reform movement.

9

Reform Communism

In 1953, at the time of Stalin's death, the Communist world consisted of regimes built on the Soviet model. In each of them the economy was based on a system of central planning. In each of them the Communist Party held a monopoly on power.[1] No political opposition was permitted. Censorship was commonly and openly practiced. Violence was part of political life both inside and outside the ruling Communist Party. Manufactured charges caused the deaths of innocent people. And over all of this presided the smiling, fatherly countenance of Joseph Stalin. Stalin wielded unchecked power. And in the other countries of the Communist world, little Stalins held sway, at least until the real Stalin in Moscow chose otherwise. Only in Yugoslavia did a Communist leader survive a break with Stalin.

Western analysts said that his was a totalitarian system--a system in which unchecked state power had entered into every nook and cranny of the land. State power, it was said, reached even into the very thoughts of the subjugated people. The pervasive ideology of communism, unchecked by the free expression of competing ideas, captured the minds belonging to the captured bodies. But in fact, the Stalinist system was inherently unstable. One of the sources of this instability was the contradiction between the very ideology it purveyed and the reality it exhibited. Communism, with its roots in the socialist tradition, contains an emancipatory message that is far removed from the oppressive atmosphere of Stalinism. In spite of it all, idealists remained. They believed in communism. And doing so, they saw the need for change.

In 1937 Leon Trotsky, the exiled leader of the left-opposition wing of the Communist Party of the Soviet Union, published a critical study of

---

1.   In some countries, as in East Germany, the Communist Party had formed "unity" parties created by alliances between Communist and non-Communist parties. But these were invariably shotgun weddings in which the Communists retained control.

the Soviet system that charged that Stalin and his supporters within the party had betrayed the Bolshevik revolution in pursuit of their own interests as a bureaucratic elite.[2] In the Soviet Union itself no such public criticism was possible. In exile in Mexico Trotsky was murdered at the orders of Stalin. But though severely repressed during Stalin's lifetime, reform voices were heard almost immediately following Stalin's death in 1953. Within the Communist Party the top leadership moved quickly. Steps were taken to abandon unfounded political prosecutions planned during the last months of Stalin's rule. Lavrenty Beria, Stalin's head of the internal security apparatus, one of the triumvirate of party leaders assuming control after the death of Stalin and a perceived threat to assume Stalin's dictatorial powers, was arrested and executed. In the initial reforms, the Party leadership sought to replace the arbitrary dictatorial power of a single individual with the rule of law and with collective leadership.

At the Twentieth Congress of the Communist Party of the Soviet Union in 1956, Party Secretary Nikita Khrushchev gave an impassioned speech in which he reviewed Stalin's crimes and located the earlier timid steps at reform within a broad proposal for de-Stalinization. Khrushchev's speech focused on Stalin's crimes against members of the Communist Party and, in particular, on the false charges against Party members during the period of the late 1930s. Many of the victims of the Stalinist era who had been sent to forced labor camps were cleared of the false charges brought against them, released, and returned--as much as possible--to their former lives. Other crimes of the Stalinist era went unmentioned. In particular, the terrible suffering inflicted on the Soviet peasantry during the period of forced collectivization remained a buried subject. Nor did Khrushchev at this time raise any questions about the twin pillars of the Soviet model inherited from the years of Stalin's rule: the centrally planned economic system and the leading role of the Communist Party derived from the Bolshevik revolution. Khrushchev's 1956 speech focused on limited reforms: the need for the rule of law and collective leadership within the Communist Party. Nevertheless, Khrushchev's speech sent shock waves throughout the Communist world. Officially secret, the speech was in fact read and discussed at all levels of the Communist Party, both within and outside the Soviet Union. Indeed, the ideas in the speech soon became well known outside the Party as well. In rejecting the infallibility of top party officials, in

---

2.   Leon Trotsky, *The Revolution Betrayed* (1937) (New York: Pathfinder, 1972).

admitting to mistakes and calling for reforms, however limited, Khrushchev raised the possibility of further reforms.

In fact, Khrushchev's revelations of Stalin's crimes at the Twentieth Congress of the Soviet Communist Party did have widespread repercussions. Until that time Communists around the world could believe, with at least some shred of plausibility, that the crimes attributed to Stalin were fabrications of a hostile bourgeois press. Khrushchev's revelations forced a historical reevaluation and launched a process of reform throughout the Communist world. The Polish Communist philosopher Leszek Kolakowski called for the primacy of individual moral conscience over party loyalty, a call echoed in East Germany by the Communist philosopher Wolfgang Harich, who went on to suggest the formation of independent unions and the supremacy of an elected parliament.[3]

In several countries, the philosophers' calls for reform were accompanied by unrest among workers. In Poland, for example, a wave of strikes followed demonstrations in Poznan in which fifty-three persons were killed. In September and October workers councils were formed in many Polish cities, causing a crisis in the leadership of the Polish Communists that resulted in the elevation of Wladyslaw Gomulka, a reformer who had been imprisoned by Stalin, to Party leadership.

In Hungary 1956 brought both calls for reform and a wave of strikes. As in Poland, workers councils were formed. In the fall the remains of Laszlo Rajk, a Hungarian Communist who fell victim to Stalin, were reburied with honor. Demonstrations surrounding the reburial of Rajk were followed by the formation of a new government headed by the Communist Imre Nagy. Under Nagy's leadership Hungary moved toward a series of reforms, including the nearly wholesale replacement of collective farms with private farms, opportunities for private businesses, and increases in wages. These economic changes were accompanied by political changes. Non-Communist political activity was permitted, and non-Communists filled high posts in the Nagy government. On November 1 Hungary announced its intention of withdrawing from the Warsaw Pact, the Soviet-dominated military

---

3. Leszek Kolakowski, "Intellectuals and the Communist Movement" (September 1956), and "Responsibility and History" (September 1957), both reprinted in Leszek Kolakowski, *Toward a Marxist Humanism* (New York: Grove Press, 1968). On Harich, see Karl Reyman and Herman Singer, "The Origins and Significance of East European Revisionism," in Leopold Labedz, ed., *Revisionism: Essays on the History of Marxist Ideas* (New York: Praeger, 1962), pp. 216-218.

alliance of Communist states. A few days later Soviet forces invaded Hungary. Seeking asylum, Nagy and officials from his government fled to Yugoslavia, where the government of Josip Tito handed them over to the Soviets. In Hungary, Soviet forces suppressed the armed opposition of the Hungarian people, forcing the formation of a more congenial Communist government under the leadership of János Kádár. A defiant Nagy refused self-criticism. In 1958 he was hanged.[4]

In general, throughout Eastern Europe reform Communists acted to replace "Stalinist" leadership with reform-minded leadership, and a public disgusted with Communist Party rule responded with both support for these limited changes and pressure for more fundamental change. Frightened by the prospects of "excessive" de-Stalinization in Eastern Europe, Soviet leadership acted to preserve Communist control in Hungary and Poland. In the period following Soviet military intervention in Hungary, Khrushchev himself retreated from his earlier attacks and called for a "balanced" view of Stalin and the system he had done so much to create.[5]

Nonetheless, the reform movement persisted. In the period following Stalin's death the immediate aim of reformers was to prevent a return to the arbitrary and violent dictatorship of a single individual. In the late 1950s and early 1960s interest in reform focused not on what might be called the pathology of Stalin's style of leadership but on institutionalized features of the Soviet system. Two features of the Soviet system were of particular concern to reformers during this time period: the economic system of central planning and the pervasive political control of artistic and cultural expression.

As we have seen, in the 1930s under Stalin's leadership the Soviet Union abandoned the mixed economy of the 1920s and moved to a system of pervasive central planning and management of all economic activity. Economic enterprises were assigned inputs produced by other enterprises, targets for production, and "customers" to whom their outputs were to be delivered by a specified time. As an incentive to enterprises, premiums were offered by the central planners for reaching

---

4. On the Hungarian uprising of 1956, see Chris Harman, *Bureaucracy and Revolution in Eastern Europe* (London: Pluto Press, 1974), pp. 124-187. On the role of the Tito government in Yugoslavia in the fate of Nagy, see Adam Westoby, *The Evolution of Communism* (New York: Free Press, 1989), pp. 246-247, 253.

5. Stephen Cohen, *Rethinking the Soviet Experience: Politics and History Since 1917* (New York: Oxford University Press, 1985), p. 107.

or exceeding targeted output.[6] Soviet leaders also appealed to the revolutionary and patriotic ardor of the workers. In 1935 the coal miner Alexei Stakhanov surpassed production norms fourteen times over in a single shift, thereby becoming a national hero of sorts.[7]

Output was initially couched simply in terms of quantity. As Soviet industry became more complex, with firms producing several different kinds of output, Soviet planners developed a system for measuring output in terms of the ruble value of gross output. However, this system, known as the VAL system, has some serious drawbacks. For one thing, in the absence of markets for consumer goods, there is no mechanism for guaranteeing that the goods that are produced are goods that consumers want. Some Western economists have argued further that in the absence of markets for inputs in the production process there is in principle no rational basis for determining the value of outputs. To the extent that this is so, a centrally planned economy is inherently unable to formulate a rational plan for the efficient use of resources.[8] Although some economists have questioned the underlying theoretical argument, in any case it is clear that the particular system of a planned economy adopted by the Soviet Union had some unfortunate economic consequences.

For example, because the premiums paid to an enterprise are determined by the gross ruble value of its output, firms have an incentive to prefer more expensive to less expensive inputs. An illustration of the economic irrationality of this incentive is provided by Viktor G. Afanasyev, who was made editor in chief of *Pravda* during the Gorbachev era. The Volga Pipe Mill

> was producing thin rolled pipe that was equal in strength to thick rolled pipe, but weighed one-half as much. Potentially the switch to such pipe could save the Soviet Union hundreds of millions of rubles and tens of

6.   Alex Callinicos, *The Revenge of History* (University Par:, Pennsylvania State University Press, 1991), p. 35, dates the introduction of wage incentives in the system of central planning to 1931.

7.   However, it now appears that this heroic feat was manufactured by having other miners do much of the work for him. Moreover, as miners in capitalist lands might expect, his effort led to the raising of production norms for other miners as well. See Marshall I. Goldman, *Gorbachev's Challenge* (New York: Norton, 1987), pp. 23-24.

8.   Ludwig von Mises, "Economic Calculation in the Socialist Commonwealth," in F. A. Hayek, ed., *Collectivist Economic Planning* (London: Routledge, 1935). Replies to Hayek's argument were offered by Oscar Lange and Fred Taylor, whose essays on this topic are reprinted in Benjamin Lippincott, ed., *On the Economic Theory of Socialism* (Minneapolis: University of Minnesota, 1938).

thousands of tons of high quality alloy steel a year. But because the Volga
Pipe Mill product sells for less, its VAL was 10 percent less and as a
consequence its wages, reserves, bonuses and all the rest of its rewards to
the producers have fallen by 15%, "fallen," but in actual fact, its labor
productivity has increased.[9]

In spite of such difficulties, the Soviet economy achieved impressive
growth rates throughout the 1930s, 1940s, 1950s, and 1960s.[10] As we
have seen, these impressive growth rates provided an attractive model of
development to many Third World countries.   Nevertheless, the
economic irrationalities of the system were apparent to some. And as the
Soviet Union developed, the task confronting the planning system
became increasingly complex, resulting in an ever-growing bureaucracy.
As early as 1956 the Soviet economist Evsei Liberman set out the basis for
a reform program aimed at introducing limited marketization, reducing
the control of central planners, and allowing enterprises to use profits for
reinvestment and for providing incentives to workers.[11] These ideas
were discussed throughout the late 1950s and early 1960s; by 1964,
experimental attempts were made to put them into practice.[12]

In the cultural sphere the reform movement was pushed along
significantly by a second de-Stalinization campaign launched by
Khrushchev at the Twenty-second Congress of the Soviet Communist
Party in October 1961. During the anniversary month of the October
revolution, daily newspapers and broadcasts riveted public attention on
"monstrous crimes" and demands for "historical justice."[13] The timing of
this de-Stalinization campaign is significant. Khrushchev and the
reformers tried to present the campaign against Stalinism as a restoration
of true Leninism. This attempt served both to provide some ideological
justification for reforms among committed Communists and to appeal to
an emotional identification with the Bolshevik revolution among the
population as a whole. The removal of Stalin's embalmed remains from

---

9.   The quotation is from M. Goldman, *Gorbachev's Challenge*, p. 22. In another
example, Goldman (p. 36) comments on the way subsidies for basic foodstuffs can produce
unwanted results: "Some peasants and farm managers still find it easier to fulfill their farm
quotas by going to the market and buying up such products as butter, milk, and meat and
passing them off as their own to the state at the higher wholesale procurement prices."

10.   Ibid., pp. 14-15.

11.   Ibid., p. 53. See pp. 51-54 for a discussion of Liberman's ideas.

12.   For an overview of the Soviet economic system, see Alec Nove, *The Economics of
Feasible Socialism* (London: George Allen and Unwin, 1983), pp. 68-117.

13.   S. Cohen, *Rethinking the Soviet Experience*, p. 111.

the mausoleum in Red Square in 1961 had a similar ideological significance.[14]

This renewed de-Stalinization initiative allowed for the public discussion of aspects of the Soviet experience that had been long repressed. The rehabilitation and release of the political victims of the Stalinist era continued at a faster pace. In 1961 the widow of Nikolai Bukharin, the murdered Bolshevik opponent of Stalin's break with the mixed economy of the 1920s, was resettled in Moscow after two decades in prison camps and reunited with the son who had been taken from her in 1937.[15] Historical and literary treatments of the labor camps appeared in officially approved publications. Artists found freedom to experiment with subjects and forms of expression that had been previously off limits.

In the early 1960s, the period of this Khrushchev "thaw," reformers within the Party and intelligentsia could look on the process of de-Stalinization with some pride and with some hope for the future. Certain limits remained. Of foremost importance, the Communist Party retained a monopoly on political power. No opposition to Communist rule was permitted.[16] And life in the Soviet Union remained hard by Western standards. Living space was limited. The variety and quality of available consumer goods lagged well behind what was common in the industrialized countries of the capitalist world. Travel and access to the outside world were restricted. But overwhelmingly, Party members, the intelligentsia, and the public at large regarded Soviet socialism as superior to Western capitalism. In the Soviet Union everyone was guaranteed a job, health care, and educational opportunity. It was only a matter of time, it seemed, until the Soviet economy surpassed the level of advanced capitalism. And given the cultural openness fostered by

---

14. Mikhail Heller and Aleksandr Nekrich, *Utopia in Power* (New York: Summit Books, 1986), p. 602, claim that this act was motivated by a power struggle within the Kremlin rather than by any concerns for justice.

15. S. Cohen, *Rethinking the Soviet Experience*, p. 79. Bukharin himself was not rehabilitated at this time in spite of the efforts of his widow and son to restore his honor. It was not until 1988 that Bukharin was officially cleared of the charges against him and his life and ideas became permissible subjects for public discussion. Cohen argues that the reason for forbidding public discussion of Bukharin was that to do so would have been to open up the possibility of a return to the NEP alternative to central planning defended by Bukharin. Cohen says that Khrushchev himself expressed regret at not having gone ahead with the rehabilitation of Bukharin.

16. Said Nikita Khrushchev, "We were scared--really scared. We were afraid the thaw might unleash a flood, which we wouldn't be able to control and which could drown us." Quoted in ibid., p. 111.

Khrushchev's reforms, there were real grounds for the hope that the remaining barriers to free expression would soon come down.[17]

But this Khrushchev thaw was not without its difficulties. The return of former prisoners presented especially delicate issues. Demanding not only restoration of what they had lost but also just punishment of those who were guilty of the crimes against them, the returnees presented a double threat to Party and government officials whose careers had been made in the Stalinist times. In many cases, the officials who had done the dirty work of arresting, interrogating, torturing, and convicting innocent persons had themselves "inherited the positions, apartments, possessions and sometimes even the wives of the vanished."[18] By the early 1960s many of these officials had advanced to relatively high posts in Party and government circles. For them the return of the vanished victims, now demanding justice, presented a personal as well as political threat.

Other of Khrushchev's reforms threatened the positions of large numbers of Party and government officials. In an effort to promote new ideas and democracy within the Party, Khrushchev mandated that a certain percentage of Party officials be replaced each year. And in an effort to streamline and decentralize the economic planning system, in 1957 Khrushchev abolished most of the major industrial ministries located in Moscow and replaced their functions with regional economic planning centers.[19]

Even though no doubt aimed at improving the quality of life for Soviet citizens, Khrushchev's reforms took on an increasingly autocratic and harebrained manner. Khrushchev would become enthused with some scheme and would impulsively act to put the scheme into motion without consulting with others in the leadership of Party and State. Thus, for example, in an effort to improve Soviet agricultural production, Khrushchev undertook a campaign to plow and sow in the previously virgin lands of Siberia. With initially promising returns from these rich virgin soils, Khrushchev greatly expanded the commitment of resources to these areas. But in the absence of fertilizers, readily available workers, machinery, roads, and storage facilities, returns from these lands fell off sharply. And in another attempt to stimulate agriculture, Khrushchev committed large tracts of Soviet land to the production of corn, which he

---

17. On Soviet economic optimism at this time, see M. Goldman, *Gorbachev's Challenge*, p. 16.

18. S. Cohen, *Rethinking the Soviet Experience*, p. 98.

19. M. Goldman, *Gorbachev's Challenge*, pp. 49-50.

had admired on his visit to the United States. Unfortunately, neither the land nor the climate of the Soviet regions was suitable for corn production. Consequently, Khrushchev's schemes resulted only in the wasting of agricultural resources.

From the point of view of many Communist Party and government officials, Khrushchev's "reforms" had gotten out of hand. His cultural thaw had provoked a host of criticisms that maligned Soviet officials and raked over old wounds. His attempted reforms of the economic system and of Party life had created chaos and uncertainty. And his increasingly high-handed style and erratic decisions menaced political life in both the Party and the State. The first period of de-Stalinization had aimed at providing stability and security for Party and government workers, all of whom wanted protection against any possible future Stalin. But in this second period of de-Stalinization, loyal Party and government officials faced instability, insecurity, and autocratic leadership as they had under Stalin. In fall 1964, while Khrushchev was vacationing at the Black Sea, Communist Party leaders decided to force his resignation.[20]

Leonid Brezhnev, who replaced Khrushchev as general secretary of the Communist Party of the Soviet Union, called for "stability of cadre," by which he meant the security of Party officials in their positions. He rescinded the Khrushchev directive regarding mandated turn-over of Party officials, and he restored the government ministries abolished by Khrushchev. Although attempts at economic reform continued throughout the Brezhnev years, the reforms were undercut by halfhearted effort and by retention of the controls of central planning agencies.[21]

In the cultural area the process of reform was actually reversed. Reform-minded editors were removed from their positions. Authors who had enjoyed some popularity in the late Khrushchev years were banned from further publication. The reform-minded historian Aleksandr Nekrich was widely criticized and expelled from the

---

20. Heller and Nekrich, *Utopia in Power*, p. 600, who are overwhelmingly critical of the entire Soviet experience, have this to say about Khrushchev: "Khrushchev was a contradictory figure, and the times during which he chanced to rule were contradictory. It is possible that Khrushchev sincerely wished to break with the Stalinist past, both his own and that of the Soviet system. By some miracle, purely human feelings and values survived in Khrushchev, feelings which for the overwhelming majority of Stalin's comrades-in-arms had been completely cast aside or effaced by the passage of time."

21. For discussion of these Brezhnev-era reforms, see Goldman, *Gorbachev's Challenge*, pp. 53-59. More significant reforms were attempted in Eastern Europe--notably in Yugoslavia, Hungary, and Bulgaria. See Nove, *Economics*, pp. 118-141; and Silviu Brucan, *The Post-Brezhnev Era* (New York: Praeger, 1983), pp. 69-71, 74-79.

Communist Party.[22] A historical work presenting the first critical study of the forced collectivization of the peasantry, planned for publication under Khrushchev, was banned under Brezhnev. Aleksandr Solzhenitsyn, who was nominated for the Lenin Prize for literature in 1964, was arrested and deported ten years later.[23] In September 1965 the writers Andrei Sinyavsky and Yuri Daniel were arrested. The writers had evaded Soviet censorship by publishing a work abroad under pseudonyms. They were convicted under a Khrushchev-era law banning anti-Soviet agitation and propaganda and were sentenced to seven- and five-year prison terms.[24] The repression of critical voices was accompanied by an affirmation of the Soviet system. De-Stalinization was replaced by a reaffirmation of the positive aspects of Stalin's leadership. By 1969 busts and portraits of Stalin were being mass produced.[25]

This termination of the process of reform, this repression of criticism, the affirmation of the Soviet system, and the revival of Stalin found significant support not only among Party and government officials with a vested interest in maintaining the status quo but also among the public at large. To a public raised under the figurehead of a benign and fatherly Stalin--honestly convinced of the fundamental legitimacy of the Soviet system and hopeful for gradual but steady improvement in the standard of living--the positive, conservative values of the Brezhnev leadership were a welcome respite from the upheavals of revolution, collec-tivization, war, and reform.[26]

However, for many of the Soviet intelligentsia, the termination of reform by the Brezhnev leadership brought an end to the hope for humane socialism. In their view the policies of the Brezhnev leadership were signs of inherent barriers to significant change in the Soviet system. They became convinced that the vested material and political interests of the ruling elite could not allow significant change. Purged from positions within the Party, government, and cultural institutions; bereft

22. S. Cohen, *Rethinking the Soviet Experience*, pp. 118-119.

23. Ibid., pp. 117-122; "Why are they prosecuting Solzhenitsyn? He is my favorite writer." So said Mikhail Gorbachev, at that time serving as the first secretary of the Stavropol District of the Communist Party. Quoted in Gail Sheehy, *The Man Who Changed the World* (New York: HarperPerennial, 1991), p. 99.

24. Heller and Nekrich, *Utopia in Power*, pp. 613-616, discuss this trial and its significance for reformers in the Soviet Union.

25. S. Cohen, *Rethinking the Soviet Experience*, p. 120.

26. Cohen claims that the overthrow of Khrushchev in 1964 probably had popular support, rooted in a longing for stability (ibid., p. 137). He also discusses "popular Stalinism," a widespread affection for the fatherly image of Stalin (p. 122).

of hope for internal reform; and abhorrent of revolutionary violence, these members of the intelligentsia were transformed from reformists to dissidents. Finding themselves outside the institutions and values of Soviet life, these individuals took a stand for basic human values. Without hope for political change, they stood, not as the conscience of the Soviet people but as moral individuals speaking to humankind at large. Their works appeared in underground, samizdat form as unpublished typed manuscripts, circulated from hand to hand within a circle of like-minded persons, or as tamizdat literature smuggled out of the USSR, published abroad, and returned to the USSR for underground circulation.

Out of the ranks of the de-Stalinizing reformers of the Khrushchev years came several prominent dissidents, among them Andrei Sakharov, Lydia Chukovskay, Aleksandr Solzhenitsyn, Pyotr Yakir, and Lev Kopelev.[27] Expelled from the Communist Party, without any political power, excluded from officially approved cultural life, and harassed by the police powers of the State, these dissidents created the beginnings of a cultural and political life outside the control of the Communist Party.

From the overthrow of Khrushchev in 1964 until the death of Leonid Brezhnev in 1982, the Soviet Union was governed by a group of Communist Party leaders who were of roughly the same age and political outlook. Like Khrushchev, they were men who came of age during the early 1930s. This was the generation that provided the leadership for the collectivization of agriculture. They were the young men whom Stalin named to replace the old Bolsheviks purged during the political trials of the late 1930s. They had risen to the top by being shrewd and loyal to their superiors. Often coming from peasant or working-class backgrounds, most of these leaders lacked much by way of formal education. They knew life from a very practical point of view. Their very lives were testimony to the transformative power of the Russian revolution. They were the upwardly mobile beneficiaries of the Soviet system. As Party officials under Stalin, they had known the fear that fell upon them as a consequence of Stalin's arbitrary and unchecked power. They supported the early Khrushchev reforms aimed at curbing such power. They favored stable, collective leadership. But they supported the Soviet system in its fundamentals. And they defended this system against radical reformers, both in the USSR and in Eastern Europe. They were the leaders who put an end to the Khrushchev thaw. They were also the leaders who sent tanks into Prague in 1968.

---

27. Ibid., p. 119.

Repression in Hungary and concessions in Poland did not put an end to reform efforts in Eastern Europe. In general, there were three primary constituencies for reform. First, workers--angered by low standards of living, attempts to impose higher production norms, and the unresponsiveness of union, government, and party officials--often resorted to the traditional weapons of the workers' movement, strikes and demonstrations, to press their demands. Sporadic attempts were made to form independent organizations, like workers' councils or unions, to represent workers' interests. Strikes broke out in East Berlin as early as 1953 and became a recurring aspect of popular pressure for reform in Eastern Europe from that time. In Poland, in particular, strikes became a leading force for political reform. There the strikes of 1956 were followed by strike waves in 1971, 1976, 1980, and 1988.[28]

A second force for reform in Eastern Europe came from the intelligentsia. Made up of students, professors, writers, artists, and journalists, the intelligentsia was primarily concerned with overcoming limitations on human rights that were common throughout the Communist world. Sometimes these demands were limited to rights such as freedom of speech, freedom of artistic creation, and freedom from arbitrary arrest, which did not directly challenge the political rule of the Communist Party. But in some cases the demand for human rights included the demand for democracy. With the emergence of organizations such as the Committee for Workers' Defense (KOR) in Poland in 1976 and Charter 77 in Czechoslovakia one year later, pressure for respect for human rights took organizational form.

A third force for reform came from within the Communist Party itself. Communists had always claimed to act for the emancipation of the working class. To be sure, the Communist Parties of the Soviet Union and Eastern Europe were riddled with opportunistic individuals whose communism was motivated more by desire for personal advancement than by altruistic identification with the working class. But many Communists were motivated by communist idealism. For such individuals the reality of workers striking, demonstrating, and sometimes fighting against Communist governments was deeply troubling. Forced to chose between the workers and the government, many Communists sided with the workers.[29]

---

28. Stanislaw Starski, *Class Struggles in Classless Poland* (Boston: South End Press, 1982), provides a view of the workers' movement in Communist Poland.

29. Stefan Heym, *Five Days in June* (New York: Prometheus Books, 1978) provides a fictional but historically informative account of the experiences of one Communist trade union leader during the uprising of construction workers in East Berlin in 1953. Adam

Communist philosophers also questioned the theoretical foundations of Soviet Marxism. In his 1923 *History and Class Consciousness*, the Hungarian philosopher Georg Lukács had argued for a humanistic Marxism that was at odds with the dialectical materialism and scientific socialism of Soviet Marxism. And although Lukács was forced to recant his views in public, he remained a force for democratizing reform within the Communist movement. He and his students were central figures in the Petofi Circle, which was a center for discussion and reform in Hungary during 1956. Lukács himself served in the government of Imre Nagy, and though he again performed self-criticism and pledged his allegiance to orthodox Communism, the influence of his alternative understanding of Marxism continued to be felt in the reform movement throughout Eastern Europe, as, for example, in the work of the Polish philosopher Leszek Kolakowski and the Yugoslav Praxis school of Marxism.[30]

These philosophical challenges to orthodox Soviet Marxism were met by government hostility and eventual repression. Kolakowski was expelled from the Communist Party of Poland, lost his teaching position, and eventually left both Poland and Marxism. In the somewhat more tolerant atmosphere of Yugoslav Communism, the Praxis school maintained an influence on culture and politics clear up to the time of the present crisis. But it did so in spite of pressure from government authorities, including expulsions from the Communist Party, restrictions on teaching and publication, police harassment, and organized ideological attacks on the members of the school.

One of the ideas developed by the Praxis school, and other Eastern European Marxists was a Marxist analysis of the Communist regimes based on the Soviet model in terms of class domination and exploitation. In this view, the Communist regimes were understood neither as socialist or communist nor as capitalist. Instead, they were understood as examples of a unique form of social organization in which

---

Westoby, *The Evolution of Communism* (New York: Free Press, 1989), p. 252, tells us that large numbers of Communist Party members did join those strikes and demonstrations.

30. In an interview, "Lukács on his Life and Work," *New Left Review*, no. 68 (July-August 1971), p. 58, Lukács comments on his participation in the Nagy government in spite of differences with Nagy. Kolakowski, *Marxist Humanism*, includes a collection of essays written while Kolakowski still considered himself a Marxist. Gerson S. Sher, ed., *Marxist Humanism and Praxis* (Buffalo: Prometheus Books, 1978), provides a collection of writings by representatives of the Praxis school. Mihailo Marković, *The Rise and Fall of Socialist Humanism* (Nottingham: Spokesman, 1975), gives an account of the thought and political significance of the Praxis school.

the upper echelons of government, enterprise management, and Communist Party constituted a ruling class that, through its control of the means of production, extracted surplus value from the working class.[31]

Whether or not a Marxist analysis of these regimes provides the most illuminating understanding of them, the existence of a privileged dominant strata was an evident aspect of the daily experience of people living in the Soviet Union and Eastern Europe. The official rhetoric of orthodox Soviet Marxism, which claimed the abolition of exploitation and the democratic rule of the working class, served only to debase Marxism and those who espoused it. In the world of what orthodox Soviet Marxists called "existing socialism," a chasm had developed between the masses of ordinary working people and the governing "Communist" elite. In the Eastern European countries, where, at least since the Hungarian uprising of 1956, Communist governments had been sustained in power by the threat of armed Soviet intervention, hostility to the governing Communist elite took on a double aspect. It was the hostility of the exploited toward their exploiters and at the same time also the hostility of a nation toward the agents of a foreign power. In countries like Poland where there was a long history of national resistance to Russian domination, nationalism became an important anti-communist force.[32]

These various pressures for reform--from workers, the intelligentsia, and idealists within the Communist Party--converged in Czechoslovakia in 1968. As a relatively advanced industrial society, Czechoslovakia had enjoyed a strong position in the trading partnerships established among the Communist bloc countries. With relaxations on trade with Western countries and development of industries elsewhere within the Communist bloc, Czechoslovakia faced increased competition and a declining rate of growth in the early 1960s. By the late 1960s Czech economists were recommending reforms that would give managers of enterprises greater autonomy. It was hoped that this would reduce inefficiencies in Czech production. These reforms threatened the positions and powers of bureaucratic functionaries who were part of the

---

31. Milovan Djilas, *The New Class: An Analysis of the Communist System* (1957) (New York: Holt, Rinehart and Winston, 1974); Georg Konrád and Ivan Szelényi, *The Intellectuals on the Road to Class Power* (New York: Harcourt Brace Jovanovich, 1979); Svetozar Stojanovic, *Perestroika: From Marxism and Bolshevism to Gorbachev* (Buffalo: Prometheus Books, 1988).

32. For a highly critical portrait of Poland's top Communists, see Teresa Toranska, *Them* (New York: Harper and Row, 1987). (published in England under the title *Oni*).

governing Communist elite. Within the Communist Party conflict developed between reformers and those who opposed the reforms. As the conflict developed, each side within the party tried to mobilize forces outside the party to its own ends. In this way both the working class and the intelligentsia were drawn into the conflict.

With the election of the reformer Alexander Dubček to the position of leader of the Czechoslovak Communist Party, the mobilized forces for reform took on a life of their own. Independent workers' councils were formed, journalists began to ignore the censors, the censors themselves demanded that their positions be abolished, and artists and intellectuals launched an open and ongoing discussion about the past and about the future of Czechoslovakia.[33] Although the government urged caution and moderation, Dubček promised to build "socialism with a human face" in Czechoslovakia. But the Prague Spring of 1968 was short-lived. In August 1968 Soviet and Warsaw Pact armed forces moved into Czechoslovakia. The reform Communists were replaced by figures who promised to restore order and to preserve a Soviet model of socialism. The nonviolent resistance of the Czech people was gradually worn down. By fall 1969, order was restored.[34]

In a sense, the Prague Spring was the last hope of utopian communism. "Socialism with a human face" named the animating goal that had motivated the whole century-long movement of European socialism. In 1968 this long-awaited "true socialism" cast its shadow on the world. After 1968 the dream was over. In Hungary the reform current of Eastern European communism continued to live in the form of experimentation with market forces and relative cultural freedom. In East Germany and Czechoslovakia the orthodox Communist world produced its most advanced industrial societies. But the relative success of these experiments in communism was clouded by comparisons with the even more prosperous neighboring Western states. In Poland serious mistakes in economic planning produced a grimly declining standard of living to which Polish workers responded with repeated waves of strikes, culminating in the formation of the independent trade union Solidarity, which would eventually successfully challenge the Communists for the political leadership of Poland. In Romania the Communist government of Nicolae Ceausescu, formed in 1965, degenerated into a personal dictatorship. In all of the countries of

---

33. Chris Harman, *Bureaucracy and Revolution*, p. 190.
34. On Czechoslovakia, ibid., pp. 188-241; and Hans-Peter Reise, ed., *Since the Prague Spring* (New York: Vintage, 1979).

Eastern Europe the Communist Party monopoly on political power was maintained in spite of increasing alienation of the government from the people. By the end of the 1960s what little popular support there had been for Communist rule had almost entirely evaporated. The threat of Soviet military intervention held the system together, but in Eastern Europe, at least, the chance for reform was lost.

10

The Fall of Communism

In Czechoslovakia in 1968 the Soviet Union proved its willingness to use military force to maintain Soviet-style socialism in Eastern Europe. The coercive threat of military intervention hung over the entire region. Short of bloody revolution, real change would have to start in the Soviet Union itself. The Brezhnev leadership, which stifled reform in Eastern Europe just as it had in the USSR, was a conservative leadership. Its fundamental aim was to preserve the Soviet system. But there were forces at work within Soviet society that made it impossible to preserve the Soviet system without change. As the economic development of the Soviet Union proceeded, readily available supplies of some resources were depleted.[1] In addition, the greater complexity of a more highly developed economy brought increasing complexity to the system of central planning. Economic growth rates declined throughout the 1970s. Food rationing was introduced in major cities in 1981-1982.[2] Such declining rates of growth eroded the confidence of the early 1960s that socialism would overtake capitalism.

Economic development also brought with it environmental problems of increasing pollution. From the factory manager to the local Party boss, leadership at all levels of the Soviet economy was pressured to increase production. With an eye to this bottom line and prohibition of independent environmentalist political action, no regard was given to the destructive environmental side effects of industrial development.

Changes were also taking place in the make-up of the Soviet people as well. The Brezhnev generation came of age in a largely peasant country with low levels of education. By the 1970s the Soviet population was overwhelmingly urban and well educated. Furthermore, with the

---

1. Marshall I. Goldman, *Gorbachev's Challenge* (New York: Norton, 1987), pp. 29-30.
2. Ibid., p. 65.

détente of the late 1960s and 1970s more and more Soviet citizens had opportunities for travel in the West. The exposure of significant numbers of educated people to the West undermined the official ideology according to which life in the capitalist world brought poverty and suffering to the masses of workers. Increasingly, young and educated Soviets saw their leaders as aged purveyors of lies.

Pervasive corruption also undermined the legitimacy of Communist Party leadership. The system of central planning made every industry dependent on political authority for the resources it needed and for the allocation of its products. With the increasing complexity of the economy, the chain of command connecting enterprises with Moscow and with one another became increasingly long. Further, within the Soviet system Party officials had considerable power over the distribution of scarce consumer goods. With the right connections an individual could get his name moved up on the list of those waiting for apartments, cars, or refrigerators. Such a system created ample opportunities for bribes, kickbacks, and payoffs. The shrewd, practical men of the Brezhnev generation had lived their whole lives within this system. They had learned to use it to the advantage of themselves, their families, and their friends. Within Communist Party and government circles distinct "mafias" developed--interconnected groups of officials who cooperated with one another to exploit positions of power for personal gain. By the end of the 1970s this corruption had become a way of life throughout much of the Soviet Union.

Like many of the leaders of the Brezhnev era, Mikhail Gorbachev was of peasant background. He was born and raised in Privolnoye, a country village of 3,300 people about 100 miles north of Stavropol.[3] Gorbachev's father was a tractor driver on a collective farm, a position of importance. His maternal grandfather was the collective farm chairman. Like the self-made men of Brezhnev's generation, Gorbachev gave his life to the Communist Party. Like most of them, he labored in obscurity as a provincial Party official (in the Stavropol District) for many years before finally being called to Moscow. Like them, Gorbachev proved his loyalty to the Party and to his superiors in the Party.

But Gorbachev was younger than the men of Brezhnev's generation. He was not himself involved in the forced collectivization of the peasantry. He was too young to have fought in the great patriotic war against German fascism. He was better educated, having had the

---

3.   Gail Sheehy, *The Man Who Changed the World* (New York: HarperPerennial, 1991), provides a biographical sketch of Gorbachev.

opportunity to study law in Moscow and there to encounter people of educated and cosmopolitan backgrounds. And he came of age during Khrushchev's initial campaign of de-Stalinization.

Gorbachev was in Moscow, studying law, when Stalin died in 1953. Zdeněk Mlynář was a young, idealistic, Czech Communist studying law with Gorbachev at Moscow State at that time. Mlynář, who went on to become a member of the Czech Prague Spring government in 1968, found many of his Russian fellow law students privately skeptical of Stalinism:

> As far as the political aspects of drinking were concerned, these were directly expressed in a symbolic ritual performed in the room I shared with six former soldiers from the front. A framed poster was hanging on the wall depicting Stalin sketching the wind-breakers on the steppes of the Volga basin on a map of the USSR, and thus, in fact, also sketching in the concrete outlines of communism. When vodka appeared on the table, the poster was turned face to the wall and the room was then dominated by an amateur portrait of a courtesan from czarist Petrograd painted on the other side. At the same time the door was locked, thus opening the door to several hours during which duplicity was unnecessary and people whose intoxicated tongues became increasingly tangled still managed to make more and more real sense.[4]

Gorbachev was not a drinker or a womanizer. But like these fellow students, he was critical of aspects of the Stalinist world around him. Mlynář, who was his friend, sat by Gorbachev's side during the showing of a film, *Cossacks of the Kuban*, which presented a grossly distorted view of life on a collective farm in the region Gorbachev knew. According to Mlynář, Gorbachev indignantly dismissed the film as "pure propaganda."[5] He is reported to have angrily denounced an anti-Semitic remark, inspired by Stalinist loyalties of the moment, by one of his fellow students. And he is also reported to have publicly protested the duplicity of privileged status for some and poverty for the many in a supposedly communist state.[6] Like Mlynář, Gorbachev was a Communist who was also an idealist. He was also, according to Mlynář, a nonauthoritarian person, a man who believed that "there can exist--

4.   Zdenek Mlynář, *Nightfrost in Prague* (New York: Karz, 1980), pp. 11-12.
5.   Sheehy, *Man Who Changed the World*, p. 74.
6.   Both incidents are reported in ibid., p. 74-75.

among communists--opponents, critics, reformers, who are not criminals."[7]

Trained in law and appointed to a Party position in the Stavropol District, Gorbachev heard Khrushchev's 1956 speech attacking Stalin when it was read to him and other Party workers by the Stavropol District Party chairman. Khrushchev's speech had a great impact on the young Gorbachev, according to a friend from his law school days.[8] For Gorbachev, as for many of his generation who came of age and entered public life at this time, Khrushchev's speech and the project of reform communism it launched became the guiding vision of his life.[9]

The overthrow of Khrushchev and the termination of reform communism presented the young reformers of Gorbachev's generation with a real setback. Many were hounded from their positions, driven from the Party, and in some cases even subjected to legal prosecution. Some left the Party in disgust. Others abandoned any dreams of reforming the system and adopted a careerist orientation. Still others, Gorbachev among them, retained their dreams but continued to work within the framework of the Communist Party.[10] Bright, articulate, hard working, loyal, and well liked, Gorbachev worked his way up the political hierarchy. In November 1978 Gorbachev moved from Stavropol to Moscow where he had been appointed to fill a vacancy as secretary for agriculture on the Central Committee of the Communist Party.

Leonid Brezhnev died in November 1982. By the time of his death the corrosive forces of economic stagnation and corruption had eaten away at public support for the regime. Dissident intellectuals, with support from the West, had succeeded in maintaining an independent and critical voice. Exposure to the West had undermined Communist criticism of capitalism and highlighted the economic failure of communism. Increasing numbers of the public had come to view Communist Party officials as corrupt, self-interested, liars, and oppressors. A large part of the population under the age of forty had become politically alienated from both the regime and the ideology of revolutionary communism.[11]

---

7.   Ibid., p. 74. See David Remnick's interview with Mlynář in the *Washington Post*, December 1, 1989, p. B1.

8.   Sheehy, *Man Who Changed the World*, p. 89.

9.   Ibid., p. 90.

10. Sheehy provides evidence of Gorbachev's sympathies for the Prague Spring in 1968 (ibid., p. 100).

11. Gail W. Lapidus, "State and Society: Toward the Emergence of Civil Society in the Soviet Union," in Seweryn Bialer, ed., *Inside Gorbachev's Russia* (Boulder: Westview, 1989), pp. 124-130.

A demoralized population responded with political apathy, absenteeism from work, petty corruption, and alcoholic drink. In these circumstances it had become apparent, even at the highest levels of the Party where the leadership was largely insulated from contact with the public, that significant reform was necessary.

Yuri Andropov, the head of the KGB, was elected to fill Brezhnev's position as general secretary of the Communist Party. Like others of Brezhnev's generation, Andropov had entered public life in the 1930s and had been rapidly promoted to fill positions vacated as a result of Stalin's purge of the old Bolsheviks in the late 1930s. As ambassador to Hungary in 1956 Andropov had presided over Soviet suppression of the reform communism of Imre Nagy and over the resulting Hungarian revolution.[12] As head of the KGB under Brezhnev, Andropov managed the arrests of prominent dissidents like Andrei Sakharov and sent torture teams to aid the Soviet war in Afghanistan.[13] But Andropov was not corrupt. And he believed in communism.

Understanding that significant reforms were needed, Andropov took several steps aimed at getting Soviet communism back on track. As head of the KGB he had assembled considerable information on corruption. As head of the Party, he initiated a campaign to cleanse the Party of corrupt elements and to stamp out corruption outside the Party.[14] In an effort to revitalize the economy, Andropov took two steps. First, he launched a moral campaign, calling upon officials, managers, and workers at all levels of the Soviet economy to work harder. This moral campaign was backed by campaigns against absenteeism and for reduction in the consumption of alcoholic beverages. Second, Andropov tried to introduce some structural changes in the economy that would allow for greater autonomy for managers of enterprises.

Although it did have some positive results, this Andropov reform program has had very limited effects. The structural economic changes were minor. More radical reform models were considered, including the increased marketization of agricultural and consumer goods as was done with considerable success in Hungary and Bulgaria.[15] But these reforms were rejected. In the end the policies accepted called for increased managerial autonomy in only two all-republic industrial ministries and

---

12. Mikhail Heller and Aleksandr Nekrich, *Utopia In Power* (New York: Summit, 1986), p. 703.

13. Sheehy, *Man Who Changed the World*, p. 139; Heller and Nekrich, *Utopia in Power*, p. 705.

14. M. Goldman, *Gorbachev's Challenge*, p. 69.

15. Silviu Brucan, *The Post-Brezhnev Era* (New York: Praeger, 1983), p. 86.

three minor republic ministries. And although the number of ministries involved was increased each year, with the basic structure of the central planning system remaining, enterprise managers lacked significant room to exercise their autonomy.[16]

Andropov's campaigns against corruption and poor work habits essentially relied on moral persuasion. Such appeals have a long history in Soviet experience, going back to the revolutionary era and Stalin's attempts to rapidly develop the Soviet economy. In the past significant numbers of Soviet citizens have responded to such exhortations. But in the climate of the post-Brezhnev era, where corruption, cynicism, apathy, and loss of faith in communism became increasingly prevalent, such moral appeals fell on largely unresponsive ears.

In any case, the death of Yuri Andropov in February 1984, after barely fifteen months in office, brought this modest effort at reform to an end. Four days after his death, Konstantin Chernenko was elected to fill the position of general secretary. Another representative of the Brezhnev generation, Chernenko made no proposal for reform during the year of his leadership. In March 1985 he died. The time had come for a new generation to provide leadership for the Party and for the Soviet Union. On March 11, 1985, Mikhail Gorbachev was elected general secretary of the Communist Party.

Gorbachev was known to be a reform Communist when he was elected to the position of general secretary. Believing in socialism and in the legitimacy of the rule of the Communist Party, Gorbachev aimed at perfecting communism rather than replacing it. His initial attempts at reform followed the lead of Andropov, who had served as something of a mentor to Gorbachev within the hierarchy of the Party. Like Andropov, Gorbachev waged a campaign to reduce the consumption of alcohol. Like Andropov, he exhorted Soviet workers to work harder. And like Andropov, he proposed relatively minor changes in the economic system. Initially, at least, *perestroika*, the restructuring that figured prominently in Gorbachev's rhetoric of reform, left the fundamental structure of central planning intact. Moreover, what changes were made were largely undercut by restrictions rooted in ideological hostility to free markets.

For example, in a 1986 law on agriculture the Soviet government announced that it would allow collective farms and state farms to sell on open markets up to 30 percent of what they produced above their plan targets. But this was in fact something that had been permitted since

---

16. M. Goldman, *Gorbachev's Challenge*, pp. 71-72.

1959. And further, this opening to markets was hemmed in by an October 1985 rule barring the sale of agricultural produce in the collective farm markets of Moscow and Georgia by anyone other than the grower himself and by a July 1, 1986, law banning "unearned" income earned from the sale of someone else's products.[17] Another provision of the 1986 law on agriculture allowed for the use of a contract brigade system on collective farms. In this system farm workers are divided into brigades of no more than ten workers. These brigades then enter into a contract with the collective farm management to produce a certain quantity of output on a stipulated tract of land. The brigade is paid bonuses for surpassing the contracted level of production. Because of the small size of the brigades, each individual has a material incentive to produce as much as possible. But again, this system was nothing really new, having been introduced near the end of Brezhnev's leadership.[18] And it, too, was hedged with ideologically motivated restrictions forbidding brigades from leasing machinery or employing labor and allowing brigades to function only under contract with collective farm management.[19]

Similarly, ideological concerns have limited changes in the law concerning the system of state-owned enterprises. Although significantly increasing the autonomy of state-owned enterprises with respect to the purchasing of materials, determination of what to produce, determination of prices, and sale of output, the law retained constraints on the ability of enterprises to respond to purely market forces. A significant sector of the economy remained under the control of the central planning model. For products falling within this sector, enterprises were directed to use specified inputs to produce specified outputs. The demands of this planned sector were often so heavy as to prevent an enterprise from significant autonomous operations. And even where production was carried on outside the central planning model, significant restrictions remained. Determination of prices was restricted by legal limits. Central governmental ministries retained a responsibility for overseeing production. Production norms remained as did norms governing the division of profits of enterprises between specified social consumption goals, like building new housing, and reinvestment in the enterprise. Further, workers in each enterprise

---

17. Ibid., p. 63, p. 76.
18. Ibid., p. 63.
19. For discussions of the law on agriculture, see Padma Desai, *Perestroika in Perspective* (Princeton: Princeton University Press, 1989), pp. 17-19, 34-38.

ultimately retained the power to override the decisions of management. For these reasons, enterprises were limited in their ability to respond to market forces.[20]

In May 1987 the central government adopted a new law on cooperatives. These "cooperatives" were, in Western terms, private businesses. In the initial framing of the law, the "cooperative" character of these private enterprises was enforced by prohibitions on the hiring of workers. Permission to work in the cooperative sector full time was limited to persons not otherwise employed in the state sector, such as students and pensioners. Further, in April 1988 a new tax law on cooperative ventures was passed that introduced a sharply progressive income tax aimed at maintaining equality of income. Clearly such measures discouraged the formation and growth of cooperatives. They reflected an underlying ideological discomfort with the whole idea of independent commercial activity that the reform law on cooperatives was originally intended to encourage. In July 1988 the law on cooperatives was revised to remove restrictions on who could form cooperatives and to permit freer business practices, including the hiring of wage laborers. In the same month the tax burden on cooperatives was reduced. These changes stimulated the development of the cooperative sector. However, ideological hostility to cooperatives remained in many localities and in much of the Soviet public, which perceived such entrepreneurial activity as inherently antisocial.[21]

In fact, the economic reforms adopted in the Soviet Union under Gorbachev were modest in comparison with economic reform policies adopted in several other socialist countries. In Hungary, China, and Bulgaria, Communist-led governments had gone much further in the direction of marketization. The limits, hedges, and restrictions on the operation of market forces that accompanied Gorbachev's *perestroika* were, of course, not by accident. They were deeply rooted in the system of values that have permeated Soviet life since the time of the Bolshevik revolution. These were values that Gorbachev, a reform Communist, had himself clearly embraced:

> To put an end to all the rumors and speculations that abound in the West about this, I would like to point out once again that we are conducting all our reforms in accordance with the socialist choice. We are looking within

---

20. Ibid., pp. 32-34.

21. Ibid., pp. 38-40; M. Goldman, *Gorbachev's Challenge*, p. 75; William Moskoff, "The Soviet Economy: The Slide to the Abyss," in Anthony Jones and David E. Powell, eds., *Soviet Update: 1989-1990* (Boulder: Westview, 1991), p. 43.

socialism, rather than outside it, for the answers to all the questions that arise. We assess our successes and errors alike by socialist standards. Those who hope that we shall move away from the socialist path will be greatly disappointed. Every part of our program of perestroika--and the program as a whole, for that matter--is fully based on the principle of more socialism and more democracy.[22]

First published in 1987, these words reflect not only a politically expedient appeal to traditional Soviet values, but also Gorbachev's own deeply held personal convictions.[23] Gorbachev's *perestroika* aimed at a restructuring, not the removal, of communism.

Similarly, Gorbachev's call for *glasnost* originated from within the project of a reform communism. As we have seen, as a law student way back in the 1950s, Gorbachev insisted on the possibility of there being differences of opinion among Communists. In calling for open, free, and frank discussion, General Secretary Gorbachev hoped to initiate a Communist pluralism in which real differences could be openly aired within a shared fundamental commitment to communist values and a communist course of development for the Soviet union.[24]

As a way of getting such a discussion going, Gorbachev renewed the de-Stalinization process of the Khrushchev years. He approved a project to create a memorial to the victims of Stalin and appointed such longtime reform advocates as the physicist and human rights activist Andrei Sakharov, the historian Roy Medvedev, and the poet Yevgeny Yevtushenko as members of the committee charged with organizing the memorial.[25] Gorbachev also appointed a number of reformers to positions as editors of various important newspapers and periodicals. Many of these men were reform Communists of Gorbachev's generation. Gannady Gerasimov, who left a position as editor of *Moscow News* to become a spokesman for the Gorbachev leadership, summed up the experience of this generation: "My generation waited in the wings far too long. We wanted to start in the 1950s. Now it's the 1990s. We spent all of our lives beating around the bush, and now this is our last chance,

---

22. Mikhail Gorbachev, *Perestroika* (New York: Harper and Row, 1987), pp. 22-23.

23. Further evidence of Gorbachev's personal commitment to the cause of socialism can be found in Sheehy, *Man Who Changed the World*, pp. 211, 263, 271, 293, 296, 355.

24. On "socialist pluralism" see Archie Brown, "Ideology and Political Culture," in Bialer, *Inside Gorbachev's Russia*, pp. 8-10.

25. Desai, *Perestroika in Perspective*, p. 74. However, Desai also points out limits on Gorbachev's *glasnost*, which as late as 1988 prohibited, among others, much of Solzhenitsyn's later (manifestly anti-Communist) works and works by Nabokov.

and that's it."[26]   But as journalists and intellectuals rather than politicians, these editors had a primary commitment to truth and freedom of expression. As the reform process progressed, journals like *Ogonyok, Argumenty i fakty,* and *Literaturnaya gazeta* provided a forum for voices that were critical of Gorbachev for not going far enough fast enough. Although launched in the service of reform communism, *glasnost,* the principle of openness, opened the door to all manner of ideas. There was nothing inherently Communist about *glasnost* and it was not long before it provided the opening for the expression of views that were frankly anti-Communist.

The process of reform encountered diverse and conflicting reactions. On the one hand, the reform process provoked forces of opposition. There were those within the Communist Party and the government who resisted reform. This resistance was motivated both by the self-interest of a bureaucracy that was threatened by change and by ideological concerns. Resistance to reform also came from the working class for whom the prospect of marketization threatened unemployment, decreasing wages and benefits, loss of subsidies for basic commodities, and rising prices.[27] On the other hand, the reform process set in motion forces for change that went far beyond the reform communism envisaged by the Gorbachev leadership. *Glasnost* opened the door to the public expression of both anticommunism and nationalism. Anti-Communists demanded an end to Communist Party rule. Nationalists demanded freedom for the republics from the control of the Soviet government. The Soviet Union was, in theory, a union of diverse peoples. In the times before the Bolshevik revolution, the tsars, seated in Russia, had extended their imperial power outward over these diverse nations. Under Stalin the Soviet Union had regained political control of the tsars' empire, though of course it was now supposed to be a fraternal union of socialist republics. But in the Baltic Republics, in the Ukraine, in Georgia, and in some of the Asian republics, nationalist aspirations for liberation from control by Moscow were rekindled by the process of reform. Nationalists and anti-Communists agreed in seeing the central governing power as their enemy. Henceforth the Gorbachev leadership faced the difficult task of trying to steer the ship of reform communism between the rocks of conservative resistance and radical reform.

---

26. Sheehy, *Man Who Changed the World,* p. 90. See pp. 8, 246, for more on the importance of this generational identity.

27. For example, Donbass coal miners and the Soviet Farmers Union each have expressed opposition to marketization. See Moskoff, "Soviet Economy," pp. 32, 37. See M. Goldman, *Gorbachev's Challenge,* p. 47.

A somewhat similar process developed in Eastern Europe, only there the forces of anti-communism and nationalism came together in hostility to indigenous puppet Communist regimes supported by the Soviet Union. In June 1988, Gorbachev endorsed the view that Soviet control in Eastern Europe violated the principle of genuine communist internationalism, which respected the right of every people to national self-determination.[28] In saying this, Gorbachev forswore any legitimate resort to force to maintain communism in Eastern Europe. In this matter Gorbachev was surely ideologically correct from the point of view of reform communism. True communism is incompatible with imperial domination. But the Eastern European response to Gorbachev's position went well beyond the reform communism he himself hoped to foster there. In a series of "bottom-up" revolutions, the people of Eastern Europe swept aside the Communist regimes that had governed them.[29]

The rapid disintegration of communism in Eastern Europe began in Poland, where, released from the threat of Soviet intervention, the independent Solidarity movement easily forced the Communist government to enter into negotiations and the formation of a coalition government, which was replaced by a completely non-Communist government when free elections finally arrived. In the years following the invasion of Czechoslovakia, Polish intellectuals had abandoned hope for building a socialist Poland. In December 1989, the newly elected prime minister, Tadeusz Mazowiecki explained that Poland must opt for capitalism because "it cannot afford to experiment."[30]

In Hungary, although there was a moment of homage to the reform communism of Imre Nagy, in March 1990 reform socialists were soundly defeated in popular elections by candidates proposed by Democratic Forum, which adopted a Christian Democratic and nationalist orientation.[31]

---

28. Carol R. Saivetz, "Foreign Policy," in Jones and Powell, *Soviet Update*, p. 119; Sheehy, *Man Who Changed the World*, p. 282, credits the historian Roy Medvedev with exposing to the Soviet public the coercive history of incorporation of the Baltic states into the Soviet Union.

29. Anthony Jones, "Introduction: The Years in Review," in Jones and Powell, *Soviet Update*, p. 5, provides an overview of the pivotal period in Eastern Europe in 1989.

30. Quoted in Daniel Singer, "After the Wall, A New Socialism?" *Nation*, 249:22 (December 25, 1989), p. 792.

31. In Budapest the remains of the martyred Communist Nagy were reburied in a memorial service that was one of the first acts of free Hungary in 1989. On this event, see the review story in the *New York Times*, March 24, 1991, sec. 1, p. 14. On the elections in Hungary, see the articles by Paul Hockenos in *In These Times*, March 21-27, 1990, p. 11, and April 18-24, 1990, p. 9.

In Czechoslovakia public indignation at police outrages against student demonstrators brought down the Communist government of Gustav Husak. In Prague, in Wenceslaus Square, hundreds of thousands cheered the appearance of Alexander Dubček, the reform Communist leader of 1968. But it was the non-Communist dissident and human rights activist Vaclav Havel who was elected president in June 1990. And under the leadership of finance minister Vaclav Klaus, Czechoslovakia followed Poland in the direction of radical free market reforms. Jan Kavan, a Prague Spring activist, explained that "they [the Husak Communists] discredited not only socialist ideals but social-democratic views too."[32]

In East Germany, reform Communists who hoped for a chance to shape an attractive alternative to capitalism were similarly swept aside in favor of the Christian Democratic politics of West German Chancellor Helmut Kohl in elections in March 1990.[33] Only in Bulgaria did reform communists win a contested election, and they were defeated one year later in October 1991.[34] Even in Albania where reform Communists for a while held control, an opposition party won in the elections of March 1992. Communism in Eastern Europe was gone. Only in Romania did a (reform) Communist regime persist.[35]

Although willing to tolerate hostile non-Communist and even anti-Communist political forces in the nations of Eastern Europe, Gorbachev was less willing to tolerate national secessionist politics in the republics of the USSR. *Glasnost* had led to the formation of opposition groups throughout the Soviet republics. In some of the republics these groups openly advocated secession from the Soviet Union. Determined to preserve the union, Gorbachev retreated from the radically democratic aspects of his reform program and tried to form an alliance with forces within the Party, the military, and the government that were committed to preservation of the union. But these were the conservative opponents of the entire reform process. In aligning himself with them, Gorbachev found himself in opposition to radical supporters of reform both within and outside the Communist Party.

---

32. On the events of 1989, see Arnost Lustig and Josef Lustig, "Return to Czechoslovakia: Snapshots of a Revolution," *Kenyon Review* 12:4 (Fall 1990), pp. 1-15. The quotation is from Paul Hockenos, *In These Times*, May 16-22, 1990, p. 11.

33. They received only 16 percent of the vote. See *Nation*, April 9, 1990, p. 475.

34. On the first Bulgarian elections of 1990, see Slavenka Drakulic, "Bulgaria's Opposition: Struggling To Be Born," *Nation* 250:21 (May 28, 1990), pp. 735-737.

35. On Albania, see Kenneth Roth, "Albanian Election Aftermath: Democracy's Race Against Fear," *Nation* 252:17 (May 6, 1991), pp. 588-591.

The reform process, with its tolerance of different points of view, had created conditions that allowed for the formation, though not yet clear legalization, of organizations independent of the control of the Communist Party.[36] Diverse grass-roots groups organized around interests ranging from ecology to rock music to home-built airplanes were formed in various locations throughout the Soviet Union. In the years between 1986 and 1988 more than 30,000 such groups were formed. In 1986 an umbrella organization, the Club for Social Initiatives, was formed in Moscow. The organizers of this club aimed at enlisting these new independent or "informal" organizations in support of Gorbachev's reforms.[37] During late summer and autumn 1987 meetings were held involving representatives of many of these informal organizations, both in Moscow and at the regional and republic levels.

In 1988 these meetings led to the formation of organizations intended to unite the various informal clubs into civic-minded umbrella organizations called Popular Fronts. These Popular Fronts were formed in various cities, regions, and republics. With their appearance the widespread grass-roots phenomenon of independently formed clubs took on a more politicized and powerful organizational form. The initiative for the formation of the various independent clubs came from the grass roots. But reform Communists played a key role in turning this grass-roots phenomenon into the Popular Front organizational form.[38] Fearful that conservative Communists would be chosen to participate in an upcoming Party conference, the reform Communists sought to use the Popular Front organizations as a way of exerting pressure on the Communist Party to continue the reform process. The reform Communists assumed that the Popular Fronts would work within the framework of the reform Communist vision; but in encouraging the formation of the Popular Front organizations, the reform Communists helped to create the organizational means by which the non-Communist and anti-Communist elements within the Popular Fronts could take independent political action.

An important point in the reform process came with the election of representatives to the Congress of People's Deputies in spring 1989. Reform Communists, this time including Gorbachev himself, again appealed to the Popular Fronts to mobilize votes for delegates pledged to

---

36. A legal ban on such organizations originated in 1932. In fall 1990 this ban was largely withdrawn. S. Frederick Starr, "Voluntary Groups and Initiatives," in Jones and Powell, *Soviet Update*, pp. 115-116.

37. Ibid., p. 100.

38. Desai, *Perestroika in Perspective*, p. 76.

continue the reform process. Even though in most places the Communist Party controlled the nominating process by which candidates were placed on the ballot, where voters were given a choice between proreform and antireform candidates, Popular Fronts were instrumental in gaining victory for supporters of reform. And in some cases where the Communist Party ran opponents of reform without permitting proreform opposition candidates to appear on the ballot, a majority of voters voted against the nominated conservative.[39]

In the Baltic Republics, Popular Front candidates won about three-quarters of the seats in the election of 1989. However, contrary to the intentions of the reform Communists, the Popular Fronts in these republics, and in some of the other republics as well, were largely committed to national liberation rather than reform communism.

A second effect of the elections of 1989 pushed the reform process beyond the bounds of reform communism. Within the Congress of Deputies, deputies representing the Popular Fronts organized themselves as the Interregional Group. Although they included Communists and formally existed as a faction within the Communist Party, these deputies in fact represented independent political forces. Under the leadership of Andrei Sakharov the Interregional Group called for the repeal of article 6 of the Soviet Constitution, which guaranteed the Communist Party the leading role in Soviet life.[40] The success of the Popular Fronts in mobilizing voters had, in fact, breached the control of the Communist Party. Following the elections, pressure mounted for legal recognition of this factual state of affairs. Throughout 1989 and 1990 independent candidates won electoral victories in local and regional elections. Independent professional associations and unions proliferated. Strikes broke out.[41] Demonstrators openly called for the end of Communist Party rule.

Many of those who were active in these independent organizations, and especially in independent political organizations, were people of the generation born in the post-war years. Leningrad journalist Elena Zelinskaya observed that "all the leaders of the informal movement [independent organizations] are people between the ages of 30 and 40." Her parents were of Gorbachev's generation, a generation that welcomed the Khrushchev thaw only to become "dissidents" during the Brezhnev

---

39. Jones, "Introduction," p. 3.
40. Sheehy, *Man Who Changed the World*, p. 293. They also opposed the appointment by the Congress of Gorbachev to the position of president of the Soviet Union, insisting that the president should be directly elected by the people.
41. Starr, "Voluntary Groups and Initiatives," p. 106.

era. Zelinskaya described them as the "crushed generation" and added that "in 1982, the last dissidents were arrested and we were alone."[42] A similar story was told by Valeria Novodvorskaya. Born in 1950, she was the daughter of dedicated Communists. She became an opponent of the system at age seventeen, during the early Brezhnev years. Arrested several times, she was placed in a mental hospital for examination and served time in prison. As a leader of the Democratic Alliance, she was one of the first to organize political opposition to the Communists. Novodvorskaya rejected Communist rule as based on an illegitimate usurpation of power. In September 1990 she was arrested for calling Gorbachev a "fascist" and "nazi criminal."[43] Novodvorskaya and Zelinskaya are typical of the leadership of the independent, or informal, organizations that formed the nucleus of an anti-Communist political movement. Younger than the reform Communists of Gorbachev's generation, they came of age after the retreat from the Khrushchev thaw. They carried with them the conviction of their formative years that communism was incapable of reforming itself. But they are not so cynical as young people in their teens and twenties who came of age during the corruption and economic decline of the late Brezhnev era.[44] Too cynical to be reform Communists but not cynical enough to be passive, it is this generation, now in their thirties and early forties, that has led the anti-Communist opposition.[45]

In November 1989, during the time of official celebration of the Bolshevik revolution, protest parades were organized in Moscow and other cities calling for an end to Communist rule.[46] On February 4 200,000 people marched through Moscow to the Kremlin walls, calling for an end to Communist rule.[47] On February 5, after heated debate, the Central Committee of the Communist Party accepted Gorbachev's

---

42. Interview by Alan Snitow, "A New Generation," *In These Times*, March 28-April 3, 1990, pp. 12-13.

43. Victor Bashkin, "Democratic Alliance: What Does It Stand For?" *Soviet Life*, April 1991; concerning the arrest, see p. 59.

44. Mikhail Ivankov, a twenty-one-year-old exception to this generalization, said of his generation: "The reality is that the majority of young people don't believe in anything." *In These Times*, May 8-14, 1991, p. 9.

45. One report (*In These Times*, May 8-14, 1991, p. 4) on a demonstration against Gorbachev by anti-Communist democrats notes that the average age of the demonstrators was around 40. Sheehy, *The Man Who Changed the World*, pp. 291, 338, also notes the crucial role of this age group in the democratic movement.

46. Jones, "Introduction," p. 14.

47. Steven L. Burg, "Political Developments," in Jones and Powell, *Soviet Update*, p. 25; Sheehy, *Man Who Changed the World*, p. 303.

recommendation that the Party voluntarily relinquish its constitutionally guaranteed leading role.[48]

With the reform movement pushing beyond the vision of reform communism, Gorbachev vacillated between support for reform and alliance with conservative Communist opposition to reform.   In supporting independence for the Baltic republics and demanding popular election of the Soviet president, the Interregional Group made it clear that its primary loyalty was to democracy rather than to communism.[49] Whereas before Gorbachev and the reform Communist leadership had assumed they could count on the support of the various informal groups, it now became apparent that out of the informals there had coalesced the basis for a radical reform challenge to the Gorbachev leadership.   In an effort to maintain political control of the reform processes, Gorbachev sought to steer a middle course between Communist Party conservatives and the radical reformers, aligning with the conservatives against the radicals and with the radicals against the conservatives.

In March 1990 Gorbachev succeeded in getting the Congress of Peoples Deputies to create the office of President of the Soviet Union for himself. As I noted, this success was achieved over the opposition of the radical democrats who demanded popular election of the president. It was followed by the formation of a Presidential Council, to which Gorbachev appointed an overwhelmingly conservative group. From the point of view of the radical reformers, these appointments were ominous. On May Day, an official Communist holiday, independent groups demonstrated in Red Square in front of the Kremlin leadership, demanding independence for Lithuania and an end to Communist rule and denouncing Gorbachev as an illegitimate president. The Gorbachev leadership responded to this demonstration by making it illegal to insult the Soviet president.[50]

A further breach between the Gorbachev leadership and the reformers came with the campaign for the presidency of the Russian Republic in May 1990. Boris Yeltsin, having been attacked by Gorbachev and driven from his position as chairman of the Communist Party in Moscow in November 1987, had remained within the Party and had by 1990 become

---

48.   Jones, "Introduction," p. 7.

49.   On the informals' support for Baltic independence, see Starr, "Voluntary Groups and Initiatives," p. 113. On support for direct election of the president, see Sheehy, *Man Who Changed the World*, p. 320.

50.   Burg, "Political Developments," p. 22.

one of the leaders of the Interregional Group.[51] His campaign for the Russian presidency in May 1990 relied heavily on the support of people outside the Party. Gorbachev threw himself against Yeltsin's election, both on the grounds that Yeltsin's proposed economic reforms would abandon socialism and on the grounds that Yeltsin's advocacy of sovereignty for the republics threatened the preservation of the union.[52] In spite of Gorbachev's campaigning against him, Yeltsin won by a narrow margin.

Yeltsin's victory against the united opposition of Gorbachev and the conservatives within the Communist Party showed that the reform movement had established a powerful electoral base outside the control of the Communist Party. It showed that it was possible for radical reformers to survive outside the Party, at least so long as they were in tune with the predominantly nationalist sentiments of their voters. In June 1990, following the election in late May, Yeltsin left the Communist Party, taking with him a number of prominent leaders of the radical-reform wing of the Party.[53]

From this point on, the process of change in the Soviet Union took on a different character. Whereas before it had appeared to be primarily a struggle between conservative and reform Communists over the future shape of the Soviet Union, it became a struggle between Communists committed to the preservation of the union and democrats willing to forsake the union in order to respect the sovereignty of the people.

In fall 1990, Gorbachev swung strongly to the cause of preservation of the union. He appointed conservatives to key positions. He sanctioned the use of lethal force to repress the independence movement in Latvia. He censored some Soviet television. And by ordering martial law he subjected numerous Soviet cities to the police presence of KGB and Soviet forces.[54]

Surveying these developments at the Congress of People's Deputies in late December 1990, Eduard Shevardnadze, the Soviet foreign minister

---

51. For an account of Yeltsin's fall in 1987, see Seweryn Bialer, "The Yeltsin Affair: The Dilemma for the Left in Gorbachev's Revolution," in Bialer, *Inside Gorbachev's Russia*, pp. 91-119.

52. Sheehy, *Man Who Changed the World*, p. 345; in fact, in May Yeltsin had come out squarely for private ownership of the land and means of production. See Alex Callinicos, *The Revenge of History* (University Park: Pennsylvania State University Press, 1991), p. 65.

53. Sheehy, *Man Who Changed the World*, p. 348; Starr, "Voluntary Initiatives," p. 110.

54. Rasma Karklins, "Nationalities and Ethnic Issues," in Jones and Powell, *Soviet Update*, p. 88; Sheehy, *Man Who Changed the World*, pp. 358-359.

and one of the leaders of Gorbachev's *perestroika*, resigned his position and warned of approaching dictatorship.

By then, however, nationalist and anti-Communist forces for change had become too strong to be easily overcome. However much Gorbachev tried to avoid a confrontation, the contending forces made such a confrontation inevitable. Even though Gorbachev succeeded in persuading the Communist Party to abandon virtually all of its ideological commitments, conservatives within the Party and the government were unwilling to give up on two key points: their control of the vast material resources of the Party and the preservation of the Soviet Union against the secessionist demands of various republics. The conflict over these two questions came to a head in summer 1991. First, under the leadership of Yeltsin the Russian Republic banned the Communist Party from maintaining its political representatives in all places of work and initiated steps to transfer worksite resources of the Party to enterprise managers.[55] Gorbachev refused to take decisive steps to overrule the republic's actions. Second, Gorbachev agreed to sign a new union treaty that would substantially increase the powers of the republics and decrease the powers of the central government.[56] Days before this new union treaty was to be signed, conservatives within the Communist Party, the government, and the military forces acted. This action was the attempted coup of August 1991.

By the time of the attempted coup the Communist Party had become a shell of its former self. Ideologically, it was on the defensive.[57] Having opened the door to independent political forces, it now faced an organized opposition with significant popular support. The Party was unprepared for this kind of struggle. Conditioned by years of authoritarian rule to passivity, and fearful of change, much of the Soviet population hung back from active participation in the reform movement. But perhaps because of this same conditioning in passivity, an effort to mobilize popular support for the preservation of a Communist Soviet Union proved a dismal failure.[58] Further, many of the most capable members of the Party had abandoned it in the last few months of the

---

55. Walter Ruby, *In These Times*, August 21-September 3, 1991, p. 3.

56. Hedrick Smith, *The New Russians* (New York: Avon Books, 1991), p. 625.

57. In a sense, what motivated the coup was not an ideological issue at all. What was at stake was not so much communism as power and preservation of the union. The coup conspirators spoke clearly for preservation of the union, but "they never invoked the name or banner of Lenin." Smith, *New Russians*, p. 624.

58.Starr, "Voluntary Groups and Initiatives," pp. 114-115.

reform process. What was left was a clique without broad support within the Party, the government, or the public at large.

Nevertheless, the coup plotters did have some resources at their disposal. In particular, they counted on the institutions of Party, government, KGB, and the military. In the struggle for the revolutionary overthrow of the tsar, Lenin had organized the Bolshevik party according to the principle of democratic centralism. As we have seen, this principle subordinated everyone in the Party to the direction of the central leadership. Under Stalin this institutionalization of centralized leadership had been extended to every aspect of Soviet life. By gaining command of the highest levels of the Party, government, KGB, and the military, the coup plotters counted on using the institutionalized authority of the center to overcome the radicalized process of reform. But this time the levers of power did not work. The "rot" of reform had penetrated too deeply within the institutions of Soviet life. Faced with the nonviolent opposition of a significant portion of the Soviet population, men at all levels within the key instruments of control--the KGB and the military--refused to obey orders. With the failure of this August coup, the more than seventy years of Communist rule in the Soviet Union came to an end.

Although Communist regimes loyal to the principles of Marxist-Leninism remain in power in China, North Korea, Vietnam, and Cuba, the processes that led to the downfall of communism elsewhere seem likely to work themselves out in these countries as well. Economic stagnation and the alienation of the Communist Party from the people have already made themselves felt to a greater or lesser degree in each of the countries in question. The remaining Communist regimes walk the earth like condemned men. It appears to be only a matter of time.[59]

---

59.   There are those--cheerleaders for the Reagan administration on the one hand and unrepentant Communists on the other--who credit the pressures exerted on the communist system by military threats and the arms race as causing the fall of communism. From the course of the discussion in this chapter, it should be clear that the deeper causes for the fall of communism are internal to its own development.

11

The Future of Socialism

The dramatic fall of communism in Eastern Europe and the Soviet Union raises questions of great political, economic, historical and philosophical significance. The Communist movement grew out of the disparity between the hope of the Enlightenment and the reality of nineteenth-century capitalism. Communists maintained that the Enlightenment dream of human emancipation could be fulfilled only by replacing capitalism with communism. In the Soviet Union the experiment was made, and communism failed. What are we to say now about the dream of human emancipation and this project of a communist alternative to capitalism?

There are those who think that the fall of Soviet communism says nothing about the possibilities of a genuinely emancipatory socialism. For many years Western Marxists have argued that the Soviet model of communism, which was copied throughout Eastern Europe and elsewhere, was a grotesque distortion of the communism of Marx and Engels and a betrayal of the socialist tradition from which Marxism sprang. From this point of view the failure of this perverted socialism has no bearing on the viability of a genuinely socialist society. Indeed, some Western Marxists hoped that the collapse of the Soviet model would create an opportunity for the advance of true socialism.[1]

By now it has become clear that no such opening to a socialist future will follow the fall of communism--at least, not in the foreseeable future. Throughout the Soviet Union and Eastern Europe, disgust with Soviet communism has brought with it distrust of all socialist experiments. It is not surprising that this is so. In March 1920, Max Weber, who was no

---

1. Among others, this view was expressed by Noam Chomsky, "Revolution of '89: The Dawn, So Far, Is in the East," *Nation*, January 29, 1990, pp. 130-133; Paul Sweezy, "Is This Then the End of Socialism?" *Nation*, February 26, 1990, pp. 257, 276; and Robin Fox, "Revolution of '89: Marxism's Obit Is Premature," *Nation*, May 14, 1990, pp. 664-666.

socialist, wrote to his friend Georg Lukács, who had joined the Bolshevik cause: "I am absolutely convinced that these experiments can only have and will have the consequence of discrediting socialism for the coming one hundred years."[2] Our examination of the fall of communism has confirmed the essential correctness of Weber's prediction.

It is entirely understandable that those who have lived through the debacle of Soviet-style communism would be psychologically disinclined to embark on some other grand socialist scheme. Nonetheless, it is not readily apparent that the failure of the Soviet-style communism does reveal a logical flaw in all possible socialisms. From a philosophical point of view, it may well be that the fall of communism is irrelevant to the possibility of a genuine form of socialism. It may well be that the defects of the Soviet model are in fact foreign to a genuine form of socialism.

Take, for example, the idea of the dictatorship of the proletariat. In Soviet Marxism, Marx's espousal of the dictatorship of the proletariat was used to justify a system in which the leadership of the Communist Party decided everything and in which basic human rights were denied. The actual proletariat, it was said, was unable to discern its true interests. Only the Party, the vanguard of the proletariat, it was said, was sufficiently farsighted to understand the course of history and to see the steps necessary to advance the true interests of the working class. Further, Soviet Communists held that within the Party it was not the consciousness of the individual Party member, occupying as he or she did a limited perspective, often corrupted by bourgeois consciousness, that embodied the consciousness of the proletariat. Rather, it was the Party as a whole, organized according to the principles of democratic centralism, that did so. Hence according to the Marxism of the Soviet model, the true dictatorship of the proletariat was the dictatorship of the Communist Party, a dictatorship that precluded the rights of all political forces outside the Party.

But in the view of Marx and Engels the dictatorship of the proletariat in fact took the form of a democratic republic, governed according to the principles of frequent elections by universal suffrage, possibility of recall of elected officials, short periods of office, and wages for officeholders

---

2.   Quoted in Arpad Kadarkay, *Georg Lukács* (Cambridge: Basil Blackwell, 1991), p. 251; in the same year, the Russian anarchist, Peter Kropotkin wrote to Lenin saying that, "If the present situation continues the very word 'socialist' will turn into a curse." Quoted by Marcus Raskin, "Rethinking the Left: The Road to Reconstruction," *Nation*, April 22, 1991, p. 512.

not to exceed wages for ordinary working people.[3] Such a dictatorship was a dictatorship only in the sense that in it the majority class, the proletariat, held the power to pass and enforce laws in its own interests.

In Lenin's own most extended theoretical discussion of the dictatorship of the proletariat, *The State and Revolution*, written in August 1917 just prior to the Bolshevik revolution, Lenin quotes from Marx's writings on the Paris Commune in which Marx lays down the principles mentioned above. Lenin also quotes a different remark of Engels: "If one thing is certain it is that our party and the working class can only come to power in the form of the democratic republic. This is even the specific form for the dictatorship of the proletariat as the Great French Revolution has already shown."[4] Although *The State and Revolution* carries a theme of the surpassing of parliamentarism with new forms of organization modeled on the soviets of Russian revolutionary experience, Lenin follows Marx and Engels in insisting that "representative institutions remain," and he contrasts the sex and property restrictions of bourgeois democracy with the expanded democracy of the dictatorship of the proletariat.[5] Lenin's theoretical conception remained rooted in the tradition of democratic Marxism. The emergence of a different sort of dictatorship--the nondemocratic dictatorship of the leaders of the Party over the whole of society--is not deeply grounded in the philosophy of Marxism. Although some pre-Marxian socialists, like Auguste Blanqui, may have envisaged such a dictatorship, most socialists have agreed with Marx and Engels in rejecting it. Many, like Kautsky and Martov, would see the dictatorship of the Soviet experience as incompatible with socialism.

An important first step on the road to this different sort of dictatorship occurred with the Bolsheviks' dismissal of the elected Constituent Assembly in January 1918. Marxists like Kautsky saw in this an unacceptable betrayal of socialism. But what was the alternative? Relinquishing power to the Assembly would have meant continuation of the war and restoration of land to the landlords, in spite of rhetoric to the

---

3.   These are principles that Marx ascribes to the Paris Commune and it is to the Paris Commune that Engels points as an example of the dictatorship of the proletariat. On the principles, see Karl Marx, *The Civil War in France* (1871) (Moscow: Progress, 1974), pp. 53-55. For Engels' claim that the Commune was a model of the dictatorship of the proletariat, see Engels' introduction in the same volume, p. 18.

4.   V. I. Lenin, *The State and Revolution* (1917) (Moscow: Progress, 1972). On Marx, see pp. 39-40; on Engels, p. 65.

5.   Ibid. On representative institutions, see p. 45; on expanded democracy, see pp. 80-81.

contrary. On these key questions the Bolsheviks did truly have great popular support. But this crucial step, the dismissal of the elected constituent assembly, undermined the institutional protection of democracy within the Soviet model.[6]

A second important step occurred with the prohibition of factions within the Communist Party adopted by the Bolsheviks in 1921. Intended as a temporary measure to prevent splits within the Party at a time of crisis, the prohibition on factions remained in place and became a fundamental principle of Party life. But such a prohibition made effective democracy within the Party impossible. Combined with psychological pressures to overcome bourgeois backgrounds, this prohibition worked to transform the "parties of the new type" into cult organizations in which individuals suppressed their own good judgment out of loyalty to the Party and the Party line.

A third step occurred with the forced collectivization of the peasantry in the early 1930s. With this step the Party knowingly set itself against the will of the vast majority of the Soviet people and committed itself to building socialism by coercive means. By these steps the conception of the postrevolutionary society as a democratic republic came to be replaced by a conception of the postrevolutionary society as a dictatorship of a revolutionary vanguard.

In one view, the oppressive nature of Soviet communism provides tragic confirmation of the fears of Engels and Plekhanov regarding the evils that would follow a premature attempt at socialism.[7] According to this view, any attempt to construct socialism on the foundations of the primitive capitalism of tsarist Russia was doomed to end with the dictatorship of a few. Because Russia lacked a highly developed economy and a large working class, a disciplined ruling elite was necessary to lead the country from feudalism to socialism. If this view is correct, the seeds of dictatorship in the Soviet model are to be found in the backward conditions of tsarist capitalism.[8] Where capitalism is

---

6. Valeria Novodvorskaya, one of the leaders of the (anti-Communist) Democratic Alliance in the Soviet Union, pointed to the fundamental significance of this step. She said, "There has been no legitimate power in this country since the Bolsheviks dispersed the Constituent Assembly." Quoted by Victor Bashkin in "Democratic Alliance: What Does It Stand For?" *Soviet Life*, April 1991, p. 60.

7. Engels (1851) writing on Thomas Münzer. Quoted in *Monthly Review*, July-August 1990, p. 52. On Plekhanov, see Jane Burbank, *Intelligentsia and Revolution* (Oxford: Oxford University Press, 1986), p. 36.

8. Among others, this view has been defended by George Konrád and Ivan Szelényi, *The Intellectuals on the Road to Power* (New York: Harcourt Brace Jovanovich, 1979); and Pavel Campeanu, *The Origins of Stalinism* (New York: Armonk, 1986).

highly developed, where economic conditions are ripe for socialism, these seeds of dictatorship would not be present. Accordingly, in this view again, the historical experience gives no reason to think that dictatorship is a necessary feature of any possible socialism.

A somewhat different reading of the historical experience, one more congenial to the Western view of Soviet Communism as the inevitable totalitarian outcome of an inherently totalitarian philosophy of Marxism, is offered by the Soviet philosopher Aleksandr Tsipko, a staff member of the Central Committee of the Communist Party of the Soviet Union. Tsipko argued that dictatorship is the likely outcome of any socialism based on the philosophy of Marxism that seeks to substitute central planning for the economic mechanisms of the market. He asked the rhetorical question: "Are stable guarantees of personal freedoms and democracy possible where all members of society work for hire for a proletarian state and have no independent sources of existence?" Tsipko answered this question in the negative. Consequently, he rejected Marxism and argued for a form of socialism that includes private ownership and free markets.[9]

Tsipko's argument lies behind the concern for "civil society" that has led many Eastern European thinkers to reject Marxism in favor of a market economy. By "civil society" they mean a layer of diverse social organizations that stand between individuals and the authority of the State, providing independent sources of power limiting the power of the State over the individual. Independent cooperatives, business firms, unions, religious and fraternal organizations, and political parties are examples of such social organizations. Tsipko's argument claimed that by doing away with private property, Marxism undermines the independence of all such organizations and hence undermines their capacity to check the power of the State. Under such conditions, he thinks, it is likely that the central offices of the State will take on dictatorial powers.

For myself, I remain unconvinced by Tsipko's argument on this point. In a system of democratic socialism the central state power need not confront a mass of unorganized individuals. Instead, between individuals and the state power there could be many layers of local and regional political organization with constitutional powers limiting higher

---

9. The quotation of Tsipko is from V. A. Riumin, "The Humanism of Economics or Economizing on Humanism?" in *Soviet Studies in Philosophy* 30:1 (Summer 1991), p. 17. See also Aleksandr Tsipko, "Was Marx a Socialist," *Soviet Studies in Philosophy* 30:1 (Summer 1991), pp. 6-13; and Aleksandr Tsipko, "The Sources of Stalinism," *Soviet Studies in Philosophy* 29:2 (Fall 1990), pp. 6-31.

levels. Further, these institutional layers could be supplemented with a variety of independent political parties and organized interest groups that, in a democratic system, could not be ignored by elected officials of the central government. Although the absence of private property might undermine the independence of these intermediate political institutions, we cannot conclude this directly from the Soviet experience, which imposed legal bans on the formation of political bodies of this kind. Neither Marxist philosophy nor the historical experience provides a good reason for thinking that a repressive political order is a necessary feature of any possible socialism.

Nevertheless, I cannot agree with those who think the fall of Soviet communism is irrelevant to the cause of socialism. The Soviet experiment in central planning has made clear the enormous practical difficulties involved in such an economic system. In a developed economy the sheer number of enterprises, and the increasing complexities of interdependence, make necessary a huge and cumbersome bureaucratic apparatus as the instrument of economic planning and control. Further, the Soviet experience suggests that a centrally planned economy is likely to be slow to respond to local problems of production, to changes in public needs, or to changing technology. Finally, the Soviet experience suggests that a centrally planned economy fails to provide the incentives necessary either for day-to-day productive effort or for innovation and development. These are difficulties that would be found in any currently foreseeable system of central planning. To the extent that this is true, the Marxist vision of a democratic, planned alternative to market economies appears unworkable. Far from being irrelevant to true Marxism, the Soviet experience--its political distortions aside--suggests at least that the Marxist vision of socialism is in fact deeply flawed.[10]

Many Western Marxists would reject this claim. They argue that in reality Marxism advocates not central planning by government bureaucracies but the democratic socialism of workers' councils. According to this alternative "council socialism," workers in every factory, mine, and office would organize themselves into a council in which they would democratically discuss and decide those questions

---

10. Alec Nove, *The Economics of Feasible Socialism* (London: George Allen and Unwin, 1983), provides an excellent, accessible discussion of the weaknesses of the classical Marxist conception of a socialist society. Nove also provides a factually informative and theoretically stimulating discussion of attempted reforms of the economic systems in Eastern Europe and China. He defends the possibility of an economic system that incorporates elements of both central planning and competitive markets.

that affect their lives. The workers at every enterprise would elect representatives to municipal and regional councils and these in turn would provide the institutional structure by which democratic socialism might be built. Not the Party nor the boss, but the workers themselves would be in charge.[11]

Such workers' councils, or "soviets," were spontaneously formed in Russia in 1917 and in other countries, notably Hungary and Germany, during the period of revolutionary transformation in Russia. In *The State and Revolution* Lenin sees in the soviets the bases for a system that would be a revolutionary democratic alternative to parliamentarism, as foreseen by Marx and Engels in their comments on the Paris Commune.[12] Some Western Marxists see the tragedy of the Russian revolution as lying in Lenin's abandonment in practice of this Marxian democratic socialism of workers' councils that Lenin had embraced in his theoretical work.

Consideration of the differences between Leninists and the council socialists raises two questions. The first concerns the historical possibility of council socialism as an alternative development for the Bolshevik revolution. The second question concerns council socialism as a vision of a possible future socialism. Consideration of the first question about the possibility of an alternative path for the Russian revolution steps outside the aim of this study. An answer to it would require a detailed knowledge of the circumstances within which the Bolsheviks found themselves and the characters of the Bolshevik leaders. It is the second question regarding council socialism as a vision of a possible future socialism that will concern us here.

I do not think the council socialist model offers a viable alternative vision of a possible future socialism. To see why this conclusion is justified, consider how council socialism would address the questions of

---

11. Among those Western Marxists who have advocated such a council socialism are: Andrew Arato and Paul Breines, *The Young Lukács and the Origins of Western Marxism* (New York: Seabury Press, 1971); Russell Jacoby, *Dialectic of Defeat: Contours of Western Marxism* (Cambridge: Cambridge University Press, 1981); Stephen Bronner, *Rosa Luxemburg: A Revolutionary for Our Times* (New York: Columbia University Press, 1987); and Alex Callinicos, *The Revenge of History* (University Park: Pennsylvania State University Press, 1991). For a discussion of the origins of council socialism as a Marxist alternative to Leninism, see Richard Hudelson, *Marxism and Philosophy in the Twentieth Century* (New York: Praeger, 1990), pp. 41-43, 200-201.

12. Lenin and council socialists agree in finding in Marx the idea that the parliamentary forms of capitalist democracy must be left behind in the socialist systems that follow capitalism. Many socialists would agree with Kautsky that Marxism does not deny the validity of parliamentary democracy for socialist countries. The interested reader should consult Marx, *Civil War in France*, which is cited by both sides in this debate.

economic life. As we saw in Chapter 1, capitalism does away with the self-subsistent units of the feudal economy. In their place, capitalism creates a vast network of interdependent agents. Such interdependencies would remain in the postcapitalist world. Coal miners would depend on steelworkers and machinists for their tools, on farmers for their food, and on textile workers for their clothing. And of course, these others would depend on the miners for the coal to heat their homes and factories. How much coal should a miner dig in a day? What tools will he use? What clothes will he wear? Where will he vacation and for how long? Who is to answer these questions? Will the miners themselves democratically resolve these issues? Then the miners dictate to the others. Council socialism must necessarily incorporate some mechanism for answering such questions. Either we introduce markets, in which case council socialism becomes a form of worker-owned cooperatives, or elected representatives of the local councils form regional and national councils by which these questions are democratically resolved. Council socialists adopt the latter of these two options. But here we seem to have returned to a system of central planning, one of the evils of "bureaucratic state socialism" for which council socialism was supposed to provide an alternative.

Council socialists would reply that what is involved here is a form of central planning that is very different from the central planning of the bureaucratic model. But precisely where does this difference lie? Defenders of council socialism see it as a radical alternative to state socialism as such. Thus, for example, Alex Callinicos chided Norberto Bobbio for thinking that parliamentary government is the only feasible form of democracy and claimed that workers' councils "represent the basis of a new form of political power capable of supplanting the existing state." It is, he said, "a distinctive combination of direct and representative democracy."[13]

In making these claims, Callinicos seems to be following the thought of Lenin in *The State and Revolution*. There Lenin sees the soviet, or council, system as a radical and more democratic alternative to parliamentary democracy. But it is not clear to me that there is any significant alternative here.

As we saw in Chapter 4, the socialists of the Second International, the socialists of the generation that followed Marx and Engels, saw parliamentary democracy as the path to socialism. They envisaged both an electoral conquest of socialism and a parliamentary form for the

---

13. Callinicos, *Revenge of History*, pp. 110, 112, 110.

construction of socialism. In this model, socialism consisted in the substitution of democratic planning for market forces. The democratic planning would be realized through parliamentary institutions and free elections. Now, does the system of workers' councils proposed by Callinicos and other Western Marxists significantly differ from the parliamentary model of the Marxists of the Second International?

Following Lenin, council socialists like Callinicos stress two fundamental differences. First, in place of the geographic units of traditional parliamentary democracy (neighborhood, city, county, state, and so on) council socialism makes workplace councils the grass-roots form of political organization. "The most distinctive feature of the soviet [workers council] as a political institution is that it is based not on any particular geographical unit, but on the workplace."[14] Second, council socialists see the system of workers councils as a "self-managed republic."[15] Third, council socialists envisage a participatory democracy entailing "the continuous and active involvement of citizens in government."[16]

Presumably the idea is that because the system is organized around the workplace, each individual will gain self-management through his or her active participation in the government of the workplace. But in fact, no such self-management will be gained. For as we saw above, because of the interdependencies of each economic enterprise, no single one of them can determine its own fate without thereby becoming a dictator to all others. Insofar as self-management is possible at all, it is only the self-management of the entire people, indirectly exercised through its elected representatives, that is truly possible. But this kind of self-management is equally possible for traditional, geographically based, parliamentary democracies.

Nor is there any plausible reason to think that council socialism will enlist the "continuous and active involvement" of every worker. For once the worker understands that fundamental decisions affecting his or her daily work life have to be made by remote representative bodies, the worker is apt to decide, wisely in my view, to leave the drudgery of daily meetings and discussions to the elected representative. In the end, the system of workers' councils proves to be no more "participatory," or "self-managed," than the parliamentary socialism of the socialists of the Second International.

---

14. Ibid., p. 110.
15. Ibid., p. 112.
16. Ibid., p. 114.

In considering what lessons we can draw from the failure of Soviet communism, I claimed that the practical difficulties experienced in the central planning of the economic system suggest that not only the Soviet model but even the democratic parliamentary model of socialism, the model embraced by the classical Marxists of the Second International, is deeply flawed. Council socialists agree with this assessment but claim to find in the model of council socialism a vision of a possible socialism that is not flawed in this way. I have tried to argue that council socialism does not offer a viable alternative to central planning. But in the course of this discussion I have touched on another vision of socialism that claims to provide an alternative to the flawed model based on the idea of central planning.

Recall that in considering how miners, farmers, and textile workers might institutionally arrange their interdependencies I hit upon two alternatives: Either they adopt market arrangements, or they adopt some variant of planning. Council socialism, like Soviet Communism and like the parliamentary visions of the Second International, opt for various forms of planning. Market socialism opts for competitive markets, rather than planning, as a way of sorting out the economic interdependencies of modern life.

Market socialists advocate a system of worker-owned cooperatives linked by market relations. Such a system is "socialist" since in it workers are not exploited by capitalists. In such a system, the workers themselves own the means of production. They also own whatever commodities they produce. Further, the workers themselves control the production process. They control the duration and pace of the working day. They choose what technology to employ. But market socialism is a market system because each of the various worker-controlled enterprises would buy its inputs and sell its outputs in competitive markets.

A market socialist system would avoid the problems that the Soviet experience suggests would be found in any system of central planning. Advocates of market socialism argue that such a system combines the efficiencies of competitive markets with the justice and democracy to which socialists have traditionally aspired. A market socialist system would also avoid the kind of criticism of state socialist systems advanced by Tsipko, because it would include the (cooperatively owned) private property necessary in Tsipko's view to prevent the political tyranny of an omniproprietary state.

Such a vision of socialism as a system of producer-owned cooperatives is also deeply rooted in the history of the socialist movement. As we saw in Chapter 2, it is to be found in the conceptions of socialism advanced by anarchists like Proudhon and also by the

Lassallean socialists in Germany. But of course, as we saw in Chapter 3, this vision of socialism was rejected by Marxists.[17] Marxists argued that were such a system to be adopted, producer-owned cooperatives would end up acting just like capitalist firms. Like capitalist firms, each cooperative would have to compete to survive. Like capitalist firms, each cooperative would have an incentive to lower its costs of production. The evils of capitalism flow, according to Marx, not from the greed of the capitalist but from the social system that pits all against all in a competitive struggle for survival.

We now know, both on the basis of theoretical investigations and on the basis of nearly forty years of practical experience with a modified version of market socialism in what was Yugoslavia, that the Marxist argument against the feasibility of market socialism is oversimplified. In some respects producer-owned cooperatives respond differently to market forces than do capitalist firms. Various proposals have also been advanced that, it is claimed, will dampen or prevent the dehumanizing tendencies of competitive markets.[18] Nonetheless, the unhappy fate of Yugoslavia, which, in addition to its disintegration into warring nationalities, suffered in its final years from high rates of unemployment like those predicted by the Marxist critique of market socialism, suggests that caution is in order before embarking on another experiment of this kind.

European social democracy offers yet another alternative to Soviet Communism that legitimately can claim deep roots in the socialist movement. In the revisionism debates of the turn of the century, Marxists of the Second International divided into two basic camps. The one remained loyal to the vision of revolutionary transformation of capitalism into a planned socialist economy. The other side in this debate favored a more moderate, evolutionary path toward socialism, one that would leave private ownership and market systems of allocation but that would try to regulate, control, and manage the economy for the good of the working class. Both visions can be found in

---

17. It is for this reason that Tsipko, in "Was Marx a Socialist?" calls for a return to pre-Marxist theories of socialism. Although Tsipko is most interested in Fourier and the Scottish socialist Robert Owen, other Soviets are rediscovering the anarchist socialist alternatives to Marxism. On the current popularity of Mikhail Bakunin, see Igor Pantin and Evgenni Plimak, "The Ideas of Karl Marx at a Turning Point in Human Civilization," in *Studies in Soviet Philosophy* 38:1 (Summer 1991), p. 49.

18. For a discussion of the market socialist alternative, see David Schweickart, *Capitalism or Worker Control?* (New York: Praeger, 1980).

the works of Marx and Engels.[19] Soviet communism offered a politically deformed realization of the vision of a centrally planned alternative to capitalism. European social democracy, of which Swedish social democracy is the clearest example, is a realization of the evolutionary, reformist alternative.[20]

But reformist socialism is not without its own difficulties. In the first place, social democracy remains profoundly undemocratic, leaving immense power over resources in the hands of the relatively small number of individuals in each country who own a disproportionate part of the means of production. Beyond this objection, social democracy itself appears to be undergoing a crisis of sorts that, if less dramatic than the crisis of communism, nonetheless must give pause to socialists eager to retreat to the banner of social democracy.[21]

In a good society workers would receive high wages, working conditions would be safe and as pleasant as possible, workers and their families would have ample opportunities for daily recreation, access to culture, and periodic vacations. The quality of the environment would be maintained. The aged, sick, and disabled would receive needed assistance. Children and their parents would be provided the resources necessary for family life to flourish. And women would not be trapped by rigid roles or impossible burdens. But in a system of international markets a country that pursues such humane goals imposes costs on its enterprises that place them at a competitive disadvantage with enterprises in other countries not subject to such costs. Capital and jobs flow to the most inhumane conditions. Further, the high taxes necessary to sustain a high level of public services encourages the flight of capital to more profitable shores. To some extent, at least, such pressures appear to be threatening traditional social democratic solutions to the problems of capitalism. With free movement across borders, socialism in one country is not possible.

Does this mean that there is no socialist alternative to capitalism? There are those who draw that conclusion. Since the fall of communism,

---

19. Boris Kagarlitsky, *The Dialectics of Change* (London: Verso, 1990), calls attention to the neglected current of reformism in Marx's work. See "Marxism and Reformism," pp. 7-55.

20. Kagarlitsky explores such themes with an eye to the history of Marxism and the problems of the present. On the Swedish model and its relation to the socialist, and specifically Marxist, tradition, see Tim Tilton, *The Political Theory of Swedish Social Democracy* (Oxford: Oxford University Press, 1990).

21. The 1991 electoral defeat of the Social Democrats in Sweden is one indicator of this crisis. The abject failure of French socialism under Francois Mitterrand is another.

much of the previously Communist world seems bent on a rapid and complete restoration of capitalist free market economies. In this it seems to me there is surprising naivete. If history has not been kind to experiments in socialism, neither has it smiled on experiments in unfettered capitalism. Both in parts of the formerly socialist world and elsewhere, in those countries that have moved closer to unfettered markets in the last decade, recent experience seems to confirm the socialists' claim that free markets lead to polarized societies in which great wealth exists side by side with great poverty.

Brazil, which has for some thirty years loyally followed the developmental prescriptions of international capitalism, has achieved a society of deep inequalities and great poverty. In the last four years 7,000 poor children have been murdered by death squads. These death squads include some police and some private forces. They are funded by private businessmen determined to reduce the shoplifting and petty theft committed by the children of the streets who are the products of Brazil's polarized economy.[22]

Since the fall of communism, much of Eastern Europe appears to be headed toward the kind of polarized economy found in Brazil. Insecurity, unemployment, and higher costs for basic commodities have already arrived, while a new class of wealthy entrepreneurs, many of them former Communists, is in the making.[23] Further, social gains won under communism--such as maternity leaves, child care centers, and abortion rights--are threatened by the corrosive effect of international competition and by reactionary political forces.[24] Following the defeat

---

22. British Broadcasting Company, "Newsdesk," December 6, 1991, 7:00-7:30 P.M. broadcast on Minnesota Public Radio. It is perhaps with such grim realities in mind that one Cuban official spoke to me in 1990 in terms of a choice between persevering on the socialist path or becoming another Venezuela, a country that is, like Brazil, deeply divided by its capitalist development.

23. From the start it was widely recognized that the change from communism to capitalism would involve hardships. As time passes, the debate in Eastern Europe between liberal free marketeers and social democrats keen on dampening the polarizing effects of the market is growing. In Czechoslovakia, Civic Forum, which led the 1989 overthrow of Communist rule, has split over this issue. *New York Times*, February 12, 1991, p. A9. In Poland half the electorate stayed home in the fall 1991 elections. Among the competing parties, the reformed Communists came in second at the polls. On the current economic difficulties facing the trailblazing experiment of the Poles in free market economics, see Daniel Singer, "Poland's New Men of Property," *Nation*, November 11, 1991, pp. 573, 590-593. For an overview on the emergence of the debate between free marketeers and social democrats in the region, see Callinicos, *Revenge of History*, pp. 60-61.

24. For a survey of the relative gains made by women under communism, see Barbara Deckard, *The Women's Movement* (New York: Harper and Row, 1983), pp. 222-237.

of the Communist government in Poland, laws were changed making abortion and divorce more difficult for women to obtain and removing women's rights to the restoration of their jobs after maternity leaves. On this last point the pressure of market forces is readily apparent. Such a right increases the costs of production. Marx's analysis of the contradictions of capitalism is not refuted by the failure of the Soviet communism.

The contradictions of capitalism do remain. Under conditions of competition, only profitable firms survive. And only those firms that keep costs down can long be profitable. Decent housing, safe working conditions, health care, family time, and a clean environment are all costly. The need for democratic control of market forces is as strong as ever. The difficulty is in seeing how this is to be done. During World War I, the socialist movement divided. One path led to the Soviet model, the other to social democracy. Social democratic solutions have met with limited success but appear to have reached a dead end. At the same time, the Soviet experience casts doubt on the viability of any nonmarket alternative to capitalism. The current crisis of socialism is rooted in the apparent failure of each of these alternatives.

But if history has roughly treated these two versions of socialism, it has not yet finished with socialism. Social democracy and Soviet Communism are branches of the socialist tree. The roots of this socialist tree lie in the moral commitment to human emancipation derived from the Enlightenment and in an awareness of the limitations of capitalism grounded in the experience of the working class. The moral imperative remains. We should not accept a world in which a majority of human beings are hungry and in need. Nor should we resign ourselves to the hope that somehow capitalism will eventually overcome this need. For we have good reasons, empirical and theoretical, to think that it never will. This judgment expresses the still valid core of the scientific understanding of capitalism derived from Marx.

Reflection on this theory of capitalism and on the historical experience of the socialist movement provides a point of departure for understanding the direction of any future socialism. For example, among other lessons the current crisis of social democracy makes clear that effective democratic control of market forces will require an international labor movement. We need international regulation of conditions of work. We need international solutions to environmental problems. We need to adopt international rules regarding the rights of workers, parents, and children. The historical experience points to the necessary ineffectualness of purely local or even national solutions to such problems. No one who has read Marx will be surprised at this.

To some extent the world has already begun to address these issues. The European Economic Community is pioneering the development of a social contract that would protect the rights of all workers within the community.   At the 1992 UN conference in Rio de Janeiro, the international community took some small steps toward the formation of international agreements to protect the environment. But clearly much remains to be done.   History has chastened socialist pretensions. Historical forgetfulness fosters capitalist illusions. Our grandparents dreamed of a better world. Our children face a future in which such a world is possible. It is up to us to make this world real.

Bibliography

Abrams, M. H. "English Romanticism." In Northrop Frye, ed., *Romanticism Reconsidered*. New York: Columbia University Press, 1963.

Appignanesi, Richard, and Oscar Zarate. *Lenin for Beginners*. New York: Pantheon, 1978.

Aston, T. H. and C.H.E. Philpin. *The Brenner Debate: Agrarian Class Structure and Economic Development in Pre-Industrial Europe*. Cambridge: Cambridge University Press, 1985.

Bashkin, Victor. "Democratic Alliance: What Does It Stand For?" *Soviet Life*, April 1991, pp. 58-60.

Berkman, Alexander. *The Russian Tragedy*. Sanday: Cienfuegos Press, 1976.

Bernstein, Eduard. *Evolutionary Socialism*. New York: Schocken, 1961.

Bialer, Seweryn, ed. *Inside Gorbachev's Russia*. Boulder: Westview, 1989.

Bowditch, John, and Clement Ramsland, eds. *Voices of the Industrial Revolution*. Ann Arbor: University of Michigan, 1978.

Boyer, Richard, and Herbert Morais. *Labor's Untold Story*. New York: United Electrical, Radio and Machine Workers of America, 1979.

Braudel, Fernand. *Capitalism and Material Life, 1400-1800*. New York: Harper and Row, 1973.

Breines, Paul. *The Young Lukács and the Origins of Western Marxism*. New York: Seabury Press, 1971.

British Broadcasting Company. "Newsdesk." Minnesota Public Radio, December 6, 1991, 7:00-7:30 P.M.

Bronner, Stephen. *Rosa Luxemburg: A Revolutionary for Our Times*. New York: Columbia University Press, 1987.

Brucan, Silviu. *The Post-Brezhnev Era*. New York: Praeger, 1983.

Buhle, Mari Jo. *Women and American Socialism*. Urbana: University of Illinois Press, 1983.

Buhle, Paul. *Marxism in the United States*. London: Verso, 1991.

Burbank, Jane. *Intelligentsia and Revolution*. Oxford: Oxford University Press, 1986.

Callinicos, Alex. *The Revenge of History*. University Park: Pennsylvania State University Press, 1991.

Campeanu, Pavel. *The Origins of Stalinism*. New York: Armonk, 1986.

Carver, George. "The Faceless Viet Cong." *Foreign Affairs* 44:3 (1966), pp. 355-356.

Caute, David. The Great Fear: The Anti-Communist Purge Under Truman and Eisenhower. New York: Simon and Schuster, 1978.

Chomsky, Noam. "Revolution of '89: The Dawn, So Far, Is in the East," *The Nation* 250:4 (January 29, 1990), pp. 130-133.

Cohen, Lizabeth. *Making A New Deal: Industrial Workers in Chicago, 1919-1939.* Cambridge: Cambridge University Press, 1990.

Cohen, Stephen. *Bukharin and the Bolshevik Revolution.* Oxford: Oxford University Press, 1980.

————. *Rethinking the Soviet Experience: Politics and History Since 1917.* New York and Oxford: Oxford University Press, 1985.

Conquest, Robert. *The Harvest of Sorrow.* New York: Oxford University Press, 1986.

Critchlow, Donald T., ed. *Socialism in the Heartland: The Midwestern Experience, 1900-1925.* Notre Dame: University of Notre Dame Press, 1986.

DeCaux, Len. *The Living Spirit of the Wobblies.* New York: International, 1978.

Deckard, Barbara. *The Women's Movement.* New York: Harper and Row, 1983.

Desai, Padma. *Perestroika in Perspective.* Princeton: Princeton University Press, 1989.

Djilas, Milovan. *The New Class: An Analysis of the Communist System.* New York: Holt, Rinehart and Winston, 1974.

Dobb, Maurice. *Studies in the Development of Capitalism.* New York: International, 1947.

————. *Theories of Value and Distribution Since Adam Smith.* Cambridge: Cambridge University Press, 1973.

Dobbs, Farrell. *Teamster Rebellion.* New York: Monad Press, 1972.

Drakulic, Slavenka. "Bulgaria's Opposition: Struggling to Be Born." *Nation* 250:21 (May 28, 1990), pp. 735-737.

Dubofsky, Melvyn. *We Shall Be All.* Chicago: Quadrangle, 1969.

Eisenhower, Dwight. *Mandate for Change.* Garden City: Doubleday, 1963.

Engels, Frederick. *Condition of the Working Class in England* (1844). London: George Allen and Unwin, 1950.

Feuer, Lewis. *Marx and Engels: Basic Writings on Politics and Philosophy.* Garden City: Anchor, 1959.

Fox, Robin. "Revolution of '89: Marxism's Obit Is Premature," *Nation* 250:19 (May 14, 1990), pp. 664-666.

Fried, Albert. *Socialism in America.* Garden City: Anchor, 1970.

Fried, Albert, and Ronald Sanders, eds. *Socialist Thought: A Documentary History.* Garden City: Anchor, 1964.

Gerrasi, John. *The Great Fear in Latin America.* New York: Collier-Macmillan, 1968.

Gilbert, Alan. *Marx's Politics.* New Brunswick: Rutgers University Press, 1981.

Gluck, Ken. "Russia's New Communists Form `Progressive' Party in Soviet CP" *In These Times,* August 21-September 3, 1991, p. 3.

Goldman, Emma. *Living My Life.* 2 vols. New York: Dover, 1970.

Goldman, Marshall I. *Gorbachev's Challenge.* New York: Norton, 1987.

Gorbachev, Mikhail. *Perestroika.* New York: Harper and Row, 1987.

Graham, Loren. *Science and Philosophy in the Soviet Union.* New York: Knopf, 1972.

Gruber, Helmut, ed. *International Communism in the Era of Lenin: A Documentary History*. Garden City: Anchor, 1972.

Hardy, Thomas. *Tess of the d'Urbervilles* (1891). New York: Dodd, Mead & Company, 1960.

Harman, Chris. *Bureaucracy and Revolution in Eastern Europe*. London: Pluto Press, 1974.

Hayek, F. A., ed. *Collectivist Economic Planning*. London: Routledge, 1935.

Heller, Mikhail, and Aleksandr Nekrich. *Utopia in Power*. New York: Summit Books, 1986.

Hellman, Lillian. *Scoundrel Time*. New York: Bantam, 1977.

Heym, Stefan. *Five Days in June*. New York: Prometheus Books, 1978.

Hilferding, Rudolf. *Finance Capital* (1910). London: Routledge & Kegan Paul, 1981.

Hinton, William. *Fanshen*. New York: Vintage, 1966.

Hobson, J. A. *Imperialism: A Study* (1902). London: Allen & Unwin, 1938.

Hockenos, Paul. "Can Hungary's Left Ressurect Itself in the Midst of a Conservative Revolution?" *In These Times* 14:17 (March 21-27, 1990), p. 11.

———. "Hungary's Free Election Defrosts Long-Latent Nationalistic Tendencies." *In These Times* April 18-24, 1990, p. 9.

———. "No Short Term Solutions for Civic Forum." *In These Times* 14:25 (May 16-22, 1990), p. 11.

Holloway, Mark. *Heavens on Earth*. New York: Liberty, 1951.

Hudelson, Richard. *Marxism and Philosophy in the Twentieth Century*. New York: Praeger, 1990.

Ilf, Ilya, and Eugene Petrov. *The Little Golden Calf*. New York: Frederick Ungar, 1961.

Jacoby, Russell. *Dialectic of Defeat: Contours of Western Marxism*. Cambridge: Cambridge University Press, 1981.

Jaffe, Philip. *The Rise and Fall of American Communism*. New York: Horizon Press, 1975.

Joll, James. *The Second International*. New York: Harper Colophon, 1966.

Jones, Anthony, and David E. Powell, eds. *Soviet Update: 1989-1990*. Boulder: Westview, 1991.

Joravsky, David. *Soviet Marxism and Natural Science*. New York: Columbia University Press, 1961.

Judd, Richard W. *Socialist Cities*. Albany: State University of New York Press, 1989.

Kadarkay, Arpad. *Georg Lukács*. Cambridge, Mass. : Basil Blackwell, 1991.

Kagarlitsky, Boris. *The Dialectics of Change*. London: Verso, 1990.

Kahn, George, and John Lewis. *The United States in Vietnam*. New York: Dell, 1969.

Kamm, Henry. "Civic Forum, Prague's Leading Party, Splits in Two." *New York Times*, February 12, 1991, p. A9.

———. "What Happened in 1956? Pick a Word." *New York Times*, March 24, 1991, sec. 1, p. 14.

Keeran, Roger. *The Communist Party and the Auto Workers' Union*. New York: International, 1980.

Kelly, Aileen. *Mikhail Bakunin*. Oxford: Clarendon Press, 1982.

Klehr, Harvey. *The Heyday of American Communism*. New York: Basic Books, 1984.

Klehr, Harvey, and John Haynes. *The American Communist Movement*. New York: Twayne, 1992.

Kolakowski, Leszek. *Main Currents of Marxism*. 3 vols. Oxford: Clarendon Press, 1978.

———. *Toward a Marxist Humanism*. New York: Grove Press, 1968.

Kollontai, Alexandra. *Selected Writings*. New York: Norton, 1977.

Konrád, Georg, and Ivan Szelényi. *The Intellectuals on the Road to Class Power*. New York: Harcourt Brace Jovanovich, 1979.

Lenin, V. I. *Imperialism, the Highest Stage of Capitalism* (1915-1916). Moscow: Progress, 1975.

———. *Marxism and Revisionism* (1908). In V. I. Lenin, *Against Revisionism*. Moscow: Progress, 1976.

———. *Our Revolution* (1923). In V. I. Lenin, *Against Revisionism*. Moscow: Progress, 1976.

———. *The Proletarian Revolution and the Renegade Kautsky* (1918). In V. I. Lenin, *Against Revisionism*. Moscow: Progress, 1976.

———. *The State and Revolution* (1917). Moscow: Progress, 1972.

Lindemann, Albert S. *A History of European Socialism*. New Haven: Yale University Press, 1983.

Lippincott, Benjamin, ed. *On the Economic Theory of Socialism*. Minneapolis: University of Minnesota, 1938.

Locke, John. *Two Treatises of Government* (1690). Cambridge: Cambridge University Press, 1963.

Lukács, Georg. "Lukács on his Life and Work." *New Left Review*, no. 68 (July-August 1971), pp. 49-58.

Lustig, Arnost, and Josef Lustig. "Return to Czechoslovakia: Snapshots of a Revolution." *Kenyon Review* 12:4 (Fall 1990), pp. 1-15.

Luxemburg, Rosa. *The Accumulation of Capital*. New York: Monthly Review Press, 1968.

———. *Rosa Luxemburg Speaks*. Edited by Mary-Alice Waters. New York: Pathfinder, 1970.

———. *The Russian Revolution*. Ann Arbor: University of Michigan Press, 1977.

Mandel, Bernard. *Samuel Gompers*. Yellow Springs: Antioch Press, 1963.

Mao Tse-tung. "Report on an Investigation of the Peasant Movement in Hunan." In *Selected Works of Mao Tse-Tung*. Vol. 1. Peking: Foreign Languages Press, 1965.

Marcuse, Peter. "Letter From the German Democratic Republic." *Monthly Review* 42:3 (July-August 1990), pp. 30-61.

Marković, Mihailo. *The Rise and Fall of Socialist Humanism*. Nottingham: Spokesman, 1975.

Marx, Karl. *Capital*. Vol. 1. New York: International, 1973.

———. *The Civil War in France.* Moscow: Progress, 1974.

———. *A Contribution to the Critique of Political Economy.* New York: International, 1972.

———. *Critique of the Gotha Programme.* Moscow: Progress, 1973.

———. *The Poverty of Philosophy.* New York: International, 1971.

———. *Value Price and Profit.* New York: International, 1974.

Marx, Karl, and Frederick Engels. *On Colonialism.* New York: International, 1972.

———. *The German Ideology* (1845-1846). New York: International, 1966.

———. *Manifesto of the Communist Party.* Moscow: Progress, 1977.

———. *Marx Engels Selected Correspondence.* Moscow: Progress, 1982.

———. *Marx Engels Werke.* Vol. 31. Berlin: Dietz Verlag, 1974.

Medvedev, Roy. *Leninism and Western Socialism.* London: Verso, 1981.

Meyer, Alfred. *Leninism.* New York: Praeger, 1967.

Miller, Richard. *Analyzing Marx.* Princeton: Princeton University Press, 1984.

Mlynář, Zdeněk. "Interview with David Remnick." *Washington Post,* December 1, 1989, p. B1.

———. *Nightfrost in Prague.* New York: Karz, 1980.

Nation (editorial statement) "Dm Über Alles." *Nation,* April 9, 1990, p. 475.

Navasky, Victor. *Naming Names.* New York: Viking, 1980.

Nove, Alec. *The Economics of Feasible Socialism.* London: George Allen and Unwin, 1983.

Ostovsky, Nikolai. *How the Steel Was Tempered.* Moscow: Progress, n.d.

Pantin, Igor, and Evgenni Plimak. "The Ideas of Karl Marx at a Turning Point in Human Civilization." *Studies in Soviet Philosophy* 38:1 (Summer 1991), pp. 42-69.

Polanyi, Karl. *The Great Transformation.* Boston: Beacon Press, 1957.

Preis, Art. *Labor's Giant Step.* New York: Pathfinder Press, 1972.

Raskin, Marcus. "Rethinking the Left: The Road to Reconstruction." *Nation* 252:15 (April 22, 1991), p. 512.

Reed, John. *Ten Days That Shook the World.* New York: Vintage, 1960.

Reise, Hans-Peter, ed. *Since the Prague Spring.* New York: Vintage, 1979.

Renshaw, Patrick. *The Wobblies.* Garden City: Anchor, 1968.

Reyman, Karl, and Herman Singer. "The Origins and Significance of East European Revisionism." In Leopold Labedz, ed., *Revisionism: Essays on the History of Marxist Ideas.* New York: Praeger, 1962.

Ricardo, David. *The Principles of Political Economy.* London: Everyman, 1962.

Riumin, V. A. "The Humanism of Economics or Economizing on Humanism?" *Soviet Studies in Philosophy* 30:1 (Summer 1991), pp. 14-41.

Robertson, Priscilla. *Revolutions of 1848: A Social History.* Princeton: Princeton University Press, 1971.

Roosevelt, Kermit. *Countercoup: The Struggle for the Control of Iran.* New York: McGraw-Hill, 1979.

Roth, Kenneth. "Albanian Election Aftermath: Democracy's Race Against Fear." *Nation* 252:17 (May 6, 1991), pp. 588-591.

Ruby, Walter. "The Unbearable Heaviness of Being Soviet," *In These Times* 15:22 (August 21-September 3, 1991), p. 9.

Rybakov, Anatoli. *Children of the Arbat.* New York: Dell, 1988.

Salvadori, Massimo. *Karl Kautsky and the Socialist Revolution 1880-1938.* London: NLB, 1979.

Salvatore, Nick. *Eugene V. Debs.* Urbana: University of Illinois Press, 1982.

Schweickart, David. *Capitalism or Worker Control?* New York: Praeger, 1980.

Sheehy, Gail. *The Man Who Changed the World.* New York: HarperPerennial, 1991.

Sher, Gerson S., ed. *Marxist Humanism and Praxis.* Buffalo: Prometheus Books, 1978.

Sholokhov, Mikhail. *And Quiet Flows the Don.* New York: Vintage, 1966.

Shore, Elliot. *Talking Socialism.* Lawrence: University Press of Kansas, 1988.

Singer, Daniel. "After the Wall, A New Socialism?" *Nation* 249:22 (December 25, 1989), pp. 790-792.

———. "Czechoslovakia's Quiet Revolution." *Nation* 250:4 (January 29, 1990), p. 122.

———. "Poland's New Men of Property." *Nation* 253:6 (November 11, 1991), pp. 573, 590-593.

Smith, Adam. *An Inquiry into the Nature and Causes of the Wealth of Nations* (1776). New York: Modern Library, 1937.

Smith, Hedrick. *The New Russians.* New York: Avon Books, 1991.

Snitow, Alan. "A New Generation." *In These Times,* March 28-April 3, 1990, pp. 12-13.

Snow, Edgar. *Red Star Over China.* New York: Bantam, 1978.

Spasowski, Romuald. *The Liberation of One.* San Diego: Harcourt Brace Jovanovich, 1986.

Starski, Stanislaw. *Class Struggles in Classless Poland.* Boston: South End Press, 1982.

Stojanovic, Svetozar. *Perestroika: From Marxism and Bolshevism to Gorbachev.* Buffalo: Prometheus Books, 1988.

Sweezy, Paul. "Is This Then the End Of Socialism?" *Nation* 250:8 (February 26, 1990), pp. 257, 276.

Taylor, A.J.P. *Revolutions and Revolutionaries.* New York: Atheneum, 1980.

Thompson, E. P. *The Making of the English Working Class.* New York: Vintage, 1966.

Thompson, Fred. *The I.W.W.: Its First Fifty Years.* Chicago: Industrial Workers of the World, 1955.

Tilton, Tim. *The Political Theory of Swedish Social Democracy.* Oxford: Oxford University Press, 1990.

Toranska, Teresa. *Them.* New York: Harper and Row, 1987.

Tristan, Flora. *London Journal* (1840). London: George Prior, 1980.

Trotsky, Leon. *The Revolution Betrayed* (1937). New York: Pathfinder, 1972.

Tsipko, Aleksandr. "The Sources of Stalinism." *Soviet Studies in Philosophy* 29:2 (Fall 1990), pp. 6-31.

————. "Was Marx a Socialist?" *Soviet Studies in Philosophy* 30:1 (Summer 1991), pp. 6-13.

Tucker, Robert. *The Lenin Anthology*. New York: Norton, 1975.

Tucker, Robert, ed. *The Marx-Engels Reader*. New York: Norton, 1978.

Tudor, H., and J. M. Tudor, eds. *Marxism and Social Democracy: The Revisionism Debate, 1896-1898*. Cambridge: Cambridge University Press, 1988.

Vishnevskaya, Galina. *Galina*. San Diego: Harcourt Brace Jovanovich, 1984.

Westoby, Adam. *The Evolution of Communism*. New York: Free Press, 1989.

About the Book and Author

The story of communism—from its historical roots in idealism to its colossal downfall in our own time—constitutes an epic of human political, social, and economic experience. In this short and gracefully written text, Richard Hudelson provides the ideal introduction to this history for readers who may know little of communism beyond what they read in newspaper headlines. Beginning with the origins of the working-class movement in eighteenth-century Britain, Hudelson encapsulates the core of the history, philosophy, politics, and economics needed to grasp the essence of communist ideology.

Throughout, Hudelson is sympathetic, yet hardly uncritical, as he emphasizes the gap between the ideals and the reality of twentieth-century communism. Readers will especially appreciate his discussion of the implications of the downfall of communism for other forms of socialism.

This is the ideal "first book" on communism—an elemental introduction that brings students to a sophisticated understanding of communism. It will prove useful for students not only of Marxism but also of political ideologies, political and social thought, social movements, and many other topics that touch upon this crucial aspect of our twentieth century.

Richard H. Hudelson is assistant professor of philosophy at the University of Minnesota at Duluth. He is author of *Marxism and Philosophy in the Twentieth Century* and many articles and reviews on Marxism and social science.

Index